2024 - 2025 Newbies Guide to

UI/UX Design Using Figma

Fundamentals of User Interface (UI) and User Experience (UX) Design Using Figma to Create User-centric Interfaces and Interactive Prototypes

ANTHONY E.
SANCHEZ

Copyright

2024 – 2025 UI/UX Design using Figma

Contents

Introduction

If you're into designs, chances are you're familiar with Figma, and its prominence is only growing. Established in 2012, this digital design and prototyping software has become a cornerstone in the design community, earning recognition from industry giants like Airbnb, Dropbox, News UK, Zoom, GitHub, Microsoft, and Notion.

Figma stands out as a collaborative, web-based design tool that facilitates real-time UI/UX development. Teams can seamlessly create prototypes from their concepts, streamlining the process of bringing ideas to fruition. It enables comprehensive visualization of models and projects, empowering professionals across various domains, including designers, product managers, and developers, to generate wireframes, prototypes, and visually striking designs.

The platform offers intuitive components for sketching graphics directly within its workspace, ensuring accessibility across all platforms. Moreover, Figma simplifies project sharing through its direct sharing capability, eliminating the need for manual exports. Unlike traditional "offline" tools like Sketch and Illustrator, where designers often have to export their work as image files for distribution, Figma allows users to share project links effortlessly.

This not only saves time but also enhances workflow efficiency. Furthermore, it fosters deeper connections between clients and colleagues by enabling them to access and review the latest version of the file directly in their browser. In essence, Figma revolutionizes collaboration in design, setting a new standard for seamless and efficient workflow management.

Why Figma?

Figma stands out as a powerhouse for collaborative design, offering a plethora of advantages that resonate particularly well with remote work dynamics. One of its key strengths lies in its seamless alignment with remote working. Figma allows team members, dispersed across the globe, to design and edit the same frame simultaneously in real time. This eliminates the need for cumbersome file transfers and ensures efficient collaboration. Similar to the collaborative features of Google Docs, Figma permits multiple individuals to work on the same document concurrently, fostering real-time discussions through integrated chats.

Moreover, Figma streamlines the sharing process by enabling the distribution of files through a single link. This facilitates easy feedback from clients and colleagues directly within the document. Such capabilities enhance workflow processes by eliminating the need to guide clients through specific areas separately, while team members can effortlessly leave comments and tag items for effective communication.

Beyond collaborative design, Figma excels in creating design systems, allowing the construction of a multitude of elements tailored to specific project needs. Designers can craft color actions, schemes, buttons, website sections, font scales, footnotes, and search bars, creating a comprehensive design repository for future use. The robust design features of Figma enable the creation and management of genuinely usable design components, proving invaluable, especially in complex projects with various streams and components.

Figma also shines in prototype design, simplifying the testing of ideas during the creative process. The platform's intuitive building approach facilitates the connection of design elements, customization of interactions, and incorporation of animations. Notably, Figma prioritizes mobile viewing, providing designers with a realistic preview of how the design will appear in real-life scenarios.

Functioning seamlessly, Figma boasts several UX design capabilities, including constraints, which allow adjustments when format dimensions change, and auto layout, enabling content to adapt to the frame's size—ideal for responsive design. Layout grids serve as templates, aiding in more efficient content formatting.

The inclusion of a version control system in Figma is a notable feature for tracking changes over time. This proves invaluable in collaborative scenarios, allowing easy rollback to previous design versions if necessary.

Furthermore, Figma offers extensive integrations with other tools such as Slack, Tello, and GitHub. This wide range of integrations simplifies the incorporation of Figma into existing workflows, enhances collaboration within teams, and streamlines overall project management.

How to Use Figma?

To begin using Figma, you only need a desktop or laptop with a reliable browser and an internet connection. Once you have these essentials, you can easily sign up for a free account on the Figma website. Once signed up, you can dive right into creating new designs. Figma allows you to craft products or projects from scratch or utilize pre-made templates. Its user-friendly editor is especially welcoming to beginners, making the design process smooth and intuitive.

UI vs UX Design in Figma

The concepts of UI and UX are often confused because they sound very similar, but there are huge differences.

UX design, or user experience design, is about designing the whole experience, and UI design, or user interface design, is about the aesthetic experience. To give this a tangible example, think about the mobile app that you use everyday, a UX designer has helped decide what features will be in the product, how they work and how you feel while you are using them. A UI designer would have also taken part in designing that mobile app, but they would have been thinking about how things look as you are using them; how much space there is between elements; how they are laid out; how much information is on each screen, and where to put things so that it is easy for users to click on.

To break it down a bit more, an experience involves a lot of different feelings, environments, actions, and reactions. On the other hand, an interface is something you make one or more interactions with, e.g a remote control with buttons on it or a microwave with switches. For instance, the UX and UI designers for Spotify, although they work closely together, the UX designer is understanding people's behavior in terms of their listening needs, come up with concepts for new ways of addressing those needs, and give them new ways to make their music listening experience easier. They are literally designing the experience of listening to music with Spotify.

While the UI designers are now taking all of that information (which is where they both somehow overlap), they are purely focused on the visual representation of those features, those new tools and those ideas, laying them out and visually representing them so that people can see how to use what they have created and get the experience the UX designer wants them to have.

In terms of tasks done by both the UX and UI designers, a UX designer starts with research, which involves understanding people (customers), then goes ahead and does some concepting, workshopping to try different ideas, coming up with different concepts to try and solve the user's problems, and finding ways to improve the user's experience.

The UI designer takes it from there and creates a clear visual representation of all of these concepts and ideas that needs to be visually laid out so a user can see what they need to do.

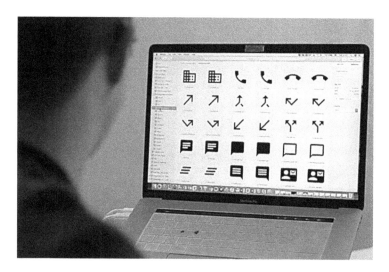

So, UX and UI designers often work on the same project and often at the same time, but they are actually responsible for very different things. And the place where the work of the UX and UI designers is really overlapping is where there is a connection between the *conceptual* and the *visual*.

A UI designer sometimes in some jobs might do a bit of conceptual wire framing before they get into the really concrete visual work, and a UX designer in some jobs (and in some companies) might be given the task of taking their concept, wireframes, and mockups into a more finished visual state, thus the confusion between both concepts of designers.

Contrasting UX and UI Designers	
UX Designers	*UI Designers*
Work with a lot of people (users and colleagues), run workshops and participate in collaborative activities.	More tasks that are just your responsibility, and you will get to sit and think and work on your own a bit more.

You look a lot more at the big picture, the big insight, and the overall view, and thus get to unravel problems.	They get to see things through to the end and put the finishing touches on everything.
This involves a lot of listening, observation, and patience, which can be really rewarding.	This involves a lot more deep focus on the detailed visual work

CHAPTER ONE
GETTING STARTED

Setting up Figma

To start out working with Figma, you will need to open an account with them. Anyone can open a free Figma account. Sign up for Figma using email, Google, or any compatible accounts. Figma will take you to the file browser when you sign up. You can locate your Drafts folder, any teams you've joined, and access to the Figma Community here. Spend some time exploring the interface. Get acquainted with the layout, tools, and features provided.

Figma offers a variety of plans to meet different needs:

- *Starter Plan*: This free plan allows you to collaborate on up to three files, each with three pages.
- *Professional Plan* ($12 per editor/month, paid annually, or $15 monthly): This subscription plan offers unlimited files and enhanced capabilities.
- *Organization package* ($45 per editor/month, payable annually): This package includes additional tools for simple cooperation across various teams and shared resources.

- *Enterprise Plan* ($75 per editor/month, payable annually): This layout is suited for large enterprises with various teams and workspaces.

Figma Interface

The Figma interface is clean and intuitive, with a design that focuses on usability. You can create wire frames, mockups and prototypes, as well as design complete user interfaces

The first thing you'll notice when entering into Figma is the File browser, which allows you to explore the contents of your account. From here, you may access your projects, resources, and teams. The file browser interface is divided into three sections: navigation, sidebar, and files.

Navigation bar: The navigation bar sits at the top of the screen and enables you to perform account-level operations.

- *User name* - This section displays the name of the currently active user. When clicked, you can switch between the accounts you are currently logged into on a certain device.
- *Search bar* - This part allows you to rapidly search for projects, files, and coworkers by name.
- *Notifications* - This is where you will see notifications about anything that happens with your account.
- *Account menu*: This is where you manage installed plugins and account settings.

Note: If you're using the Figma desktop software, you can simply move between projects and the file browser; projects open in new tabs, while the file browser is identified by the Home icon.

Sidebar: This is the interface area that appears on the left side of the screen. It enables you to navigate between files and prototypes.

- *Recents* - In this tab, the files and prototypes you've recently viewed or updated appear first.
- *Drafts* - Here you can see all of the draft variations you've created. You will also find the Deleted tab, which allows you to see archived data. Right-clicking on the file will reveal the options to restore or permanently remove previously erased data.
- *Community* - Here you may browse files and plugins posted by other Figma users. We will come back to this part in our next blog post.
- *Teams* - This page lists all of the teams to which you belong.

Files - this section displays all of your files. You can select how the files are shown on each page of the File Browser: as a grid or as a list. By default, the grid view is enabled. Files can be filtered and arranged based on your needs. There are buttons to add files above the list of files in the *Recents* and *Drafts* tabs: new design file or new FigJam file. Each file format has a unique collection of features and tools. Design files will allow you to construct your own interface designs. FigJam files are digital whiteboards that can be used for various purposes, including online meetings and seminars.

Familiarize yourself with Figma's file browsing interface before proceeding to open your first project. Press the New Design File button.

File Interface

The four sections that make up your Figma user interface when editing a file are the Canvas, Toolbar, Layers panel, and Properties panel.

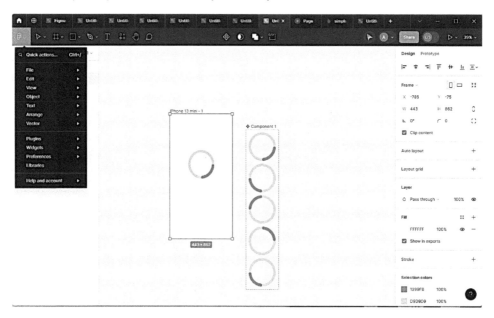

Canvas

The major area is the canvas, which is in the white center of the screen. This is your workspace. All of your design assets, including pictures, vectors, mock-ups, gifs, illustrations, and so forth, are grouped together on this background.

The canvas's default backdrop color is decided by your current theme: light or dark. In light mode, the default background color of newly generated files is #F5F5F5, which is a light gray. In dark mode, they will default to the off-black color #1E1E1E. The background color of new pages is determined by the background color of the current page, not by your theme. To change the background color, deselect any layers and use the color picker in the backdrop section of the right sidebar.

Toolbar

The toolbar is a bar located at the top of the screen. Here, you will discover all of the tools and functionalities you need to develop interfaces. The main menu allows you to access a list of all Figma functions. The list also includes keyboard shortcuts.

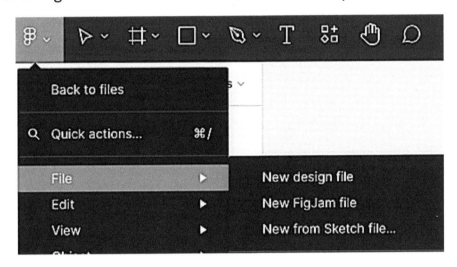

❖ *Note*: All keyboard shortcuts can be viewed in a separate panel. To enable it, navigate to the *Main menu > Help and Account > Keyboard shortcuts*.

Figma menu

The Figma menu enables you to work with the file, its objects, vectors, texts, plugins, and more in a variety of ways. You can, for instance, access the plugins and widgets, alter the display, and export the file's parts.

- *Quick action* – Enables you to search for the names of different functions.

- *File* – Enables you Save and Export files.
- *Edit* – Here you'll discover basic file editing functions like Copy, Paste, Undo, and Redo, as well as advanced object selection functions.
- *View* – It has functions for zooming and moving within a file, and it gives you control over how Grids and Rulers appear.
- *Object* – Provides with necessary functions to work with objects.
- *Text* – Enables you format text (Alignment, Bold, Italics) and create numbered and bulleted lists.
- *Arrange* – Enables you to organize and place objects using many Distribute and Align functions.
- *Plugins* – Installed plugins can be managed here. Plugins improve the functionality of Figma and facilitate the design process.
- *Integration* – Enables you share your designs with applications that are connected.
- *Preferences* – This is where you adjust Figma's settings for selecting element's visibility and dragging objects.
- *Libraries* – This consist of styles and components that can be used in your file.

Move and Scale tools – The Move tool enables you move objects around the Canvas and reorder layers in the panel, while the Scale tool enables you to resize the layers without having to distort them.

Frame and Slice tools – The Frame *tool* allows you to select the screen size you will be working on. On the other hand, Slice tool enables you to export a certain part of the screen into a new layer.

Vector elements – this section has the Place image function and simple geometric shapes.

Pen and pencil tools – Two tools that let you construct vector components from scratch. The pen tool can be used to create custom shapes. The pencil tool lets you include hand-drawn graphics.

Text tool – used to create text layers

Resources – A novelty. Figma's resources, including components, plugins, and widgets, can be accessed straight from the toolbar.

Hand tool – enables you to navigate your project and click within a file without accidentally selecting and moving objects.

Comment tool – enables you to quickly communicate ideas to team members.

Components – Functionality that allows you to convert various graphic elements into components. Components are "parent" layers, with multiple "children". Each offspring shares the same design characteristics as its parent. To get all the children to adopt the new properties, you just need to change their parents.

Masks and selections – Two capabilities that allow you to control the overlay relationship between several design elements.

Editing objects – Enables you to alter a vector by adding different elements including backgrounds, curves, colors, breakpoints, and new segments.

Conversation – Make group calls and collaborate with others on your Figma file.

Spotlight – The Spotlight function is accessible via your profile symbol. It lets you recommend users to follow you on the canvas.

Presentation – By using the presentation mode, you can project your image into a frame. Models can be shown virtually on a variety of devices, including tablets, MacBooks, and iPhones.

Share – This feature allows you to share the whole Figma file. You will have control over the various limitations that permit users to either change or just view the file.

> **Note:** When working in a team, you can engage observation mode by clicking on another user's avatar and tracking their movements in real time. When the Observation mode is enabled, a colored frame will appear around the tracked user's canvas and avatar. To make it easier for your teammates to keep track of your activities, you can also increase your visibility. Tap on your avatar and then select Spotlight me.

Zoom/view options – enables you quickly adjust the view option of the file.

Left sidebar

Layers panel

The section of the screen on the left is the layers panel. This is where the file's layers and components will all be visible.

This is where you will find all of the things you have added to the canvas. Every object is a distinct layer. You will see an icon next to each layer that represents its category. Double-click on a chosen layer in the Layers panel to change its name.

Note: Although it's difficult to remember to change the names of default layers, try as much as you can. This will in turn enable you to locate a specific piece in your file more easily and maintain file organization. Still, nothing is lost if you manage to forget about it. You may tidy up the mess by using plug-ins like "Clean Document."

Every layer has lock and unlock options. To do this, mouse over the layer name and click on the Padlock icon that shows up next to it. Because they will be denoted with an appropriate icon, locked or invisible layers will be easy to identify from other levels.

The ability to lock layers is really handy, especially when a number of them occupy the background. This helps you to avoid accidentally moving elements. Additionally, you have the option to turn the selected layers' visibility ON/OFF. Click the Eye icon to perform this. The layers list makes it easy to distinguish between locked and disabled layers because the appropriate icons are used to indicate their status.

Assets

This tab displays the components that can be used in your file. These could be buttons, icons, or other intricate UI components. Employ the search box to locate a particular part. You can search the libraries that are available to you as well as the current file for components.

Page

Each file can have an infinite number of pages added to it. With a separate canvas backdrop for every page, you can create multiple prototypes within a single file.

You can change the Layers panel's width. To do this, click and hold the panel's right border. Your pointer will be converted to a white double arrow. After that, drag the edge to the desired width.

Properties Panel

The section on the right side of the screen is called the Properties panel, and it has three tabs: Design, Prototype, and Inspect.

Design - Here you can inspect and edit the properties of all layers, including frames, shapes, and words.

Prototype - This tab contains the prototype's settings and connections to other parts in the file. The graphic elements can be used to create animations and interactions.

Inspect - This tab demonstrates how to code the specific items in your project. There are three forms available: CSS, Android, and iOS.

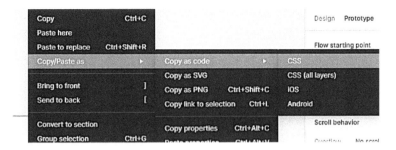

Frames vs Groups

Grouping is simply putting different objects into a single layer that can be managed. In other words, every object in the group will get moved about as one, get scaled as one and get resized as well. There are a few ways to group objects together, either by clicking on the layer panel and tapping *Group Selection*, using the **Ctrl + G** shortcut, or by doing it manually from the canvas by click-dragging your cursor across to select the objects and then right-clicking to select the Group Selection option.

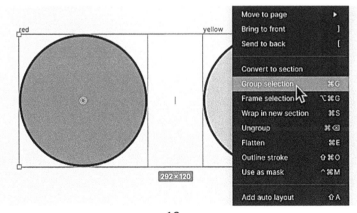

One unique thing you can do when handling groups is to define the spacing of the objects by clicking on each layer of the object and adjusting them accordingly. So essentially, in groups, you don't have a lot of control over, let's say, constraints or flex properties, as we would soon see with frames, but grouping does give you a basic level of control in terms of being able to scale things around and move them.

The second layer management method that is available in Figma is Framing. To do this, similar to how the grouping was done, ensure you have the object selected, either through the layer's panel or by doing a click and drag across to select all the objects. Afterwards, right click on the layer's panel, and click Frame Selection. Now, all the objects will get put together in one single layer called Frame.

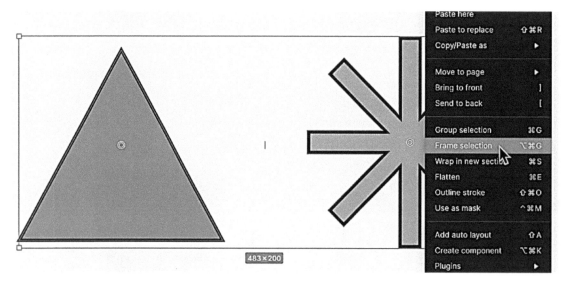

The first difference with respect to grouping is that the symbol on the layer panel is slightly different. However, most importantly, if you try to resize the frame, nothing happens to the object within it.

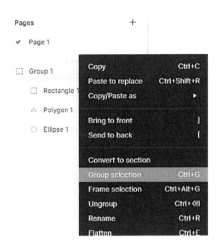

Meanwhile, in grouping, the object automatically scales and resizes in proportion to the changes. Now, this is happening because, in frames, unlike in groups, there is a little more complexity when it comes to how we define the relationship between the objects inside the frame. However, such scaling issues with framing are easily addressable when you click on the Resize to fit option in the Design panel on the left side of your screen, and that would make sure that the frame adjusts to fit the range of the object.

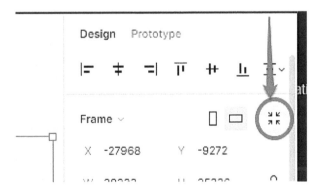

In frames, there are constraints that essentially dictate how you want the object to position itself based on changes in the width or height adjustments of the frame. If you are in the context of product design, you will have objects within frames that are continuously dynamically resizing. For instance, if you have a cross device application that has been rendered across multiple screen sizes and dimensions and you want to essentially dictate how the very same interface is going to behave across those different adjustments, Frames is a tool that can help you achieve that, especially when you are defining a breakpoint or an initial frame to get started with.

CHAPTER TWO
WORKING WITH LAYERS

Parent, Children and Siblings

We use these phrases to describe how objects interact with one another on the canvas. Parents are objects, specifically frames, components, and groups, that hold other objects. Children are elements/objects that exist within the parent. Siblings are elements/objects that exist within the same parent.

We use these phrases to describe how objects interact with one another on the canvas. Parents are objects, specifically frames, components, and groups, that hold other objects. Children are items that exist within a parent. Siblings are items that exist within the same parent. Any objects inside a frame are children, and the frame itself is the parent. A frame by itself does not constitute a parent. It is only considered a parent if it contains objects. If a parent has more than one object, their child's objects are considered siblings. Objects such as frames, groups, and components, can function as both parents and children.

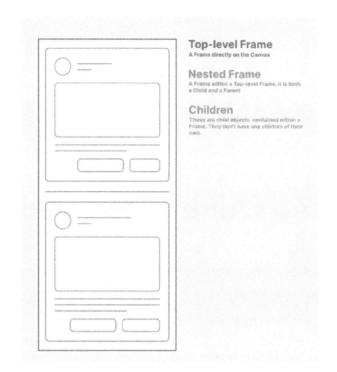

Top-level Frame
A Frame directly on the Canvas

Nested Frame
A Frame within a Top-level Frame. It is both a Child and a Parent

Children
These are child objects contained within a Frame. They don't have any children of their own.

Parent-child interaction

While these concepts are not expressly used in the product, they are necessary for understanding how objects behave and interact with one another in Figma. Unlike their biological counterparts, they act as containers (parents) and contents (children), influencing one another. As opposed to a clearly established lineage with obvious inheritance.

Properties

There are parent-child relationships that entail influence. The parent is almost always going to be a frame.

The following properties can be added to a frame to effect all of its child objects:

- *Layout Grids*: Develop visual structure for your design.
- *Auto Layout*: Generate dynamic frames that react to their contents.
- *Clip Content*: Hide any objects that extend beyond the Frame's limits.

You can also add properties to a child object.

- *Constraints*: Define how child items will respond when resizing the parent Frame.

Parent behavior

When you move an object on the canvas, Figma will determine whether or not to re-parent it. Re-parenting indicates that the object is removed from its current parent and nested within another parent object. For example, you could shift an object from one parent frame to another. When you add new items to a frame in Figma, it follows the same parenting logic.

The default behavior is:

- If an object is smaller than a frame, it will become a child of the frame.
- If an object is bigger than a frame, it cannot be made into a child element

However, this default behavior can be bypassed:

- When bringing in an element/object on the canvas, press and hold down the space key to prevent Figma from re-parenting it.
- Likewise, when moving an element/object out of the boundaries of a frame, press and hold down the Space key to keep the element/object within the current parent control.

Alignment, Rotation, and Position

Each element you add to the canvas, be it a form, text object, or image, gets its own layer. This enables you to change each layer independently while creating coherent and complicated designs. The majority of these attributes are located at the top of the Design panel in the right sidebar. A lot of these parameters can also be adjusted directly on the canvas.

❖ *Note that the alignment, position, and dimensions of auto layout frames differ from the options mentioned above.*

Alignment

Alignment tools allow you to position layers on the canvas relative to one another. Figma will align your layers based on your individual picks.

- Select an object or layer, and Figma will align it to its parent. This could be the contained frame of a component, a group, or a frame.
- Select multiple layers: Figma will align layers in reference to one another, their parent frame, or the selected layers in an instance.

To align an object with its parent layer or to align many objects with one another, use the alignment controls located in the right sidebar:

|⊨   -   Align left

╪   -   Align horizontal centers

=| -   Align right

⫟   -   Align top

╫   -   Align vertical centers

⫡   -   Align bottom

Alternatively, keyboard shortcuts can be used

Action	Keyboard shortcut
Align Left	Alt + A
Align Horizontal centers	Alt + H
Align Right	Alt + D
Align Top	Alt + W
Align Vertical centers	Alt + V
Align Bottom	Alt + S

Hold down Shift and click the alignment buttons to align many elements in a group to their parent frame.

Snap to settings

When resizing an item, changing layers, or shifting vector points, use the snap to settings to help them line with other components on the canvas. As a visual cue, a red guide emerges on the painting.

- *Snap to geometry*: Only used in vector editing mode. When this option is enabled, clicking and dragging a vector point will align it with other vector points.
- *Snap to objects*: Align the outermost and center points of various objects.
- *Snap to pixel grid*: Align items to an underlying grid to avoid pixel misalignment when exporting elements. This setting works regardless of whether the pixel grid is visible.

To enable and disable Snap in settings, open a Figma design file and navigate to the Figma menu, then Preferences. These settings are also accessible via the Quick Actions menu.

Snap-to-Settings is applied throughout your Figma design files. If *Snap to geometry* or *Snap to objects* are enabled, hold **Ctrl** to temporarily disable them.

To temporarily disable Snap to pixel grid with **Ctrl**, ensure you're in vector edit mode and zoomed in on the canvas. To determine if you've zoomed in sufficiently, activate the pixel grid (**Shift'**) and zoom in until the grid is visible. It is important to note that this shortcut does not require the pixel grid to be enabled.

Tip – If you've enabled **Ctrl+click** to open right-click menus, click and hold the element before clicking Control to temporarily stop snapping. This avoids mistakenly activating the secondary menu.

Distribute

Use distribution to ensure that layers in a selection have equal spacing. You must have many layers or objects selected.

Distribute will cause Figma to maintain the locations of the outermost objects or layers:

- Distribute horizontal spacing: the items or layers on the far left and far right will remain in place.
- Distribute vertical spacing: both the top and bottom objects or layers will remain in place.
- Tidy up (smart select).

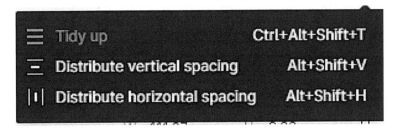

Tidy up

Use tidy up to rapidly align layers in one dimension as columns or rows, or combine columns and rows to create two dimensional layouts. Smart selections then allows you to modify the distance between the objects in your selection both vertically and horizontally.

Based on what you select, you will be able to see one of the following:

- Tidy up vertical selection (one-dimension)
- Tidy up horizontal selection (one-dimension)

o Tidy up (two-dimension)

One dimensional selections – Figma will organize objects according to the axis on which they overlap when the selection is made on either the vertical or horizontal axis (one dimension). Those on the X axis will have their horizontal spacing modified, whereas those on the Y axis will simply have their vertical spacing adjusted. Figma will set the Space Between value based on the most common spacing in the selection.

> *Note: Figma will not automatically align the objects along both axes when you use tidy up on a one-dimensional selection; nevertheless, you can utilize the alignment tools in the right sidebar I to make any additional modifications.*

Two dimensional selection - When applying tidy up to two-dimensional objects, such as a grid, the method is significantly more stringent. Figma adjusts both the horizontal and vertical distances between things.

The horizontal and vertical spacing will be determined by their beginning positions and may be the same or different. Once Figma cleans up the layers, you can modify the vertical and horizontal spacing. Unlike distribute, which repositions things inside the confines of the original selection, tidy up organizes all objects into a grid that corresponds to the top-left corner of your selection.

Position

Layers in the canvas can be moved in any of two directions or axes: horizontally (X axis) and vertically (Y axis). Figma uses X and Y coordinates to represent the position of a layer on the canvas. These are the top-left corners of the layer's boundaries. Open the Design panel on the right sidebar. Use the X and Y fields to change the layer's coordinates. To easily alter the X and Y coordinates, use the fundamental mathematical formulae $- + * / \char`^ ()$. You can place an equation before or after an existing value, or you can completely replace it with a new equation.

> *Note: If you rotate a layer in the canvas, Figma will base the X and Y coordinates of that layer on the original top-left corner of the layer's bounds.*

Nudge layers

To nudge your layers' positions, use the arrow keys. You can configure two default nudge amounts in Figma: small nudge and big nudge. By default, the little nudge is set to 1 and the big nudge is set to 10. Both of these values occur in resolution-independent points.

Adjust your selection with the arrow keys. The arrow keys will utilize your small nudge settings; hold down Shift to use the large nudge settings instead.

Dimensions

Each layer on the canvas will have its own proportions. To view the proportion of the layer:

- o Select the layer from the canvas or layers panel.
- o Examine the dimensions found in the blue label situated beneath the bounding box of the layer.
- o You can also see the proportions of any layer in the right sidebar by utilizing the W and H fields.

To modify the dimensions of a layer, first select it. There are then several methods:

- To change the width of a layer, hover over its left or right borders until it displays. To resize, just click and drag.
- To change the height of a layer, hover over the top or bottom limits until they show. Click and drag to resize.
- To change the width and height of a layer, hover over any corner of its limits until it displays. Click and drag to resize.
- Adjust the W and H fields in the right sidebar.

Constrain proportions

The button enables you to constrain the layer's dimensions to the current percentage. This parameter may be found in the right sidebar, close to the dimension settings (**W** and **H**). When this option is enabled, Figma will keep the layer's original width-to-height ratio if you resize it in the sidebar. Figma updates the other field correspondingly if you modify one of the **W** or **H** fields.

Tip – Hold down the Shift key when drawing to make flawless squares, circles, and polygons. Figma will enable the restrict proportions option in the right sidebar.
By default, Figma draws shapes from the top-left corner. You can draw a shape from the center by holding down the **Alt** or **Option** key.

Rotation

Rotate individual layers, such as objects, groups, and frames, or a subset of layers. Figma will rotate your selection around its horizontal and vertical centers. The default rotation for each layer you add to the canvas is 0°. Your selection can be rotated 180° in both directions:

- A positive angle moves counterclockwise, towards 180°.

o   A negative angle moves clockwise, approaching -180°.

Once you reach 180° in either direction, Figma will count down to 0° in that direction. For example, moving 15° past 180° yields an angle of -165°.

Right sidebar
In the right sidebar, you can find the rotation field near the top of the Design panel.

o   Choose the object(s) or layer(s) you want to rotate.
o   Use the rotation ⌐ 0° field to input the rotation you want on the right sidebar.

Canvas
1.   Hover just beyond one of the layer's boundaries to see the icon emerge.
2.   Click and drag to rotate your selection.
   ▪   Drag clockwise to achieve a negative angle (approaching -180°).
   ▪   Drag counterclockwise to generate a positive angle (approaching 180°).
3.   Hold down the Shift key to snap rotation values in 15-point increments.

Note: Figma will not rotate any effects that have been applied to a layer or selection.

Flip layers
The Flip horizontal and Flip vertical transformations are another option for replicating rotating layers. To do a flip transformation, use either the right-click menu or the keyboard shortcuts – **Shift + H** to **Shift + V** to Flip Vertical.

Lock and Unlock Layers

Layers can be locked to avoid unintentional modifications or to prevent them from being moved about the canvas. When you lock a layer, you cannot interact with it or move it around on the canvas. You can still choose a locked layer in the Layers Panel and change any of its parameters. If you lock a parent frame or group, all of its child levels will likewise be locked. It is impossible to unlock kid layers without first unlocking the parent.

> ❖ *Note: The right-click menu allows you to select locked layers. Right-click on the layer, then click Select Layer from the menu. A padlock icon is placed next to each locked layer.*

There are three ways locking and unlocking layers can be done:

- *Keyboard*: The keyboard shortcut for this is **Ctrl + Shift + L**.
- *Canvas*: While doing it on the Canvas, require that you simply right-click on the layer, select Unlock or Lock from the list of options.
- *Layer panel*: Hover over a layer in the Layers Panel to make the lock appear. Click the padlock to lock the layer. Figma will lock the padlock next to that layer in the Layers Panel. If this is a group or frame, all of its children will be locked. You will no longer be able to alter the layer in your canvas. To unlock the layer, simply click the padlock again.

 Tip – Multiple layers can be locked and unlocked at once. Click on the lock icon and drag across the different layers you want to work on.

Hide and Rename Layers

Layer's Visibility

The Layers panel allows you to toggle a layer's visibility. You can still alter the position or characteristics of a hidden layer. The visibility of layers is indicated by an eye icon. This visibility can be toggled in two ways:

- o *Keyboard shortcut* – Simply click **Ctrl + H**
- o *Layers panel* – You can toggle each layer individually or conceal all child element in a frame or group. Simply, hover over the layer, frame or group in the layers panel. Then, click on the eye icon to toggle visibility OFF. This will cause the layer to be hidden right in the canvas, and this will also be indicated in the layers panel by being grayed out as inactive. Hit the eye icon again to toggle ON visibility.

When a layer is hidden, it cannot be selected in the canvas. This involves navigating to the right-click menu and using the Select layer option. Using the Layers panel and displaying outlines, you may still pick the layer.

Rename Layers

Having a well-defined naming system or hierarchy aids layer management in your files. The Rename layer tool lets you swiftly rename numerous layers at once.

Layer modal can be renamed in a number of ways:

- o Select the particular layer from the layer's panel or canvas
- o Right-click and choose Rename, or use the keyboard shortcut – **Ctrl + R**

This will cause the Rename Layers Modal to open just above the canvas.

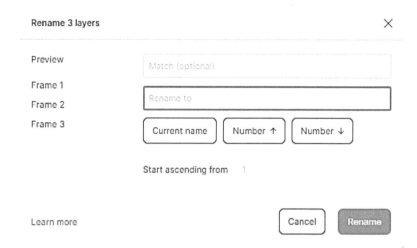

Tip – You can rename a single frame or flow beginning point directly from the canvas by double-clicking its present name.

<u>Rename Bulk Layers</u>

If you wish to simply rename the selected layers, enter the desired name into the *Rename to* field and click Rename. However, it's more probable that you'll want to give each layer a somewhat different name so that you can distinguish things in the layers panel.

There will be some buttons underneath the *Rename to* field. When clicked, these buttons add a specific code to the *Rename to* field, allowing you to generate slightly different names for each layer.

- o The current name button indicates the layer's current name.
- o The Number ↑ button adds a number to each layer's name, in ascending order.

o The Number ↓ button adds a number to each layer's name in descending order.

<u>Renaming layers with the same name</u> – First select the layers to rename. Then, do the keyboard shortcut; **Ctrl + R** to have the Rename Layer Modal open up. Now, enter a fresh name in the *Rename to* field.

<u>Renaming layers with numerical suffix</u> - If you want a group of similar layers to have the same name but be distinct, you can add a number to the end (or beginning) of the layer's name.

CHAPTER THREE
WIREFRAMING

What exactly is a Wireframe?

A wire frame is a digital outline of your design that represents the big picture of an idea. In other words, they are the outline and bare bones of the key elements of a design. Put simply, it is a two-dimensional drawing of a page interface that is used to define and plan the information hierarchy on a page or screen, in other words, how should the items on the page be organized? What content goes where? How should space be allocated? And what functionalities are available, which include positioning elements such as buttons, menus, and headings.

The purpose of a wireframe is to help the designer plan how everything is laid out on the screen before they get bogged down in the nitty-gritty details of the design. It also provides a basic artifact that can be tested with users to confirm or deny different design choices.

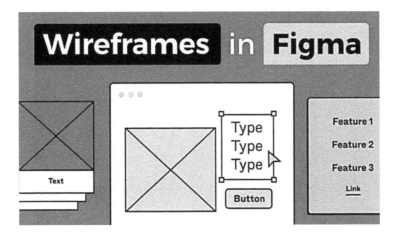

Imagine you are designing a mobile app. Before you decide on the perfect colors and design aesthetic, you will create wireframes for each basic screen.

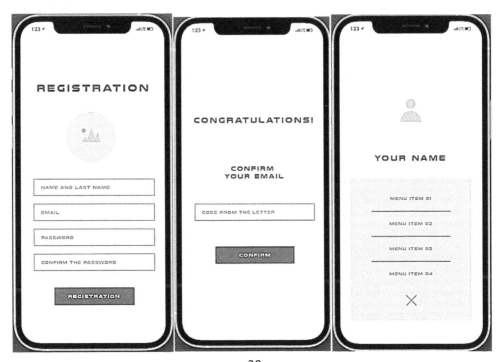

This will help you plan out exactly how the user will undertake tasks, engage with key elements and navigate through your products or app.

Types of Wireframes

Traditionally, there are two types of wireframes – the Physical Hand-drawn sketch and Digital wireframes. A hand drawn sketch is made simply by using paper, pens, and markers, and a digital wireframe can be made using Figma. Whether a hand-drawn sketch wireframe or a digital wireframe, they are both made up of the same things; basic fundamental shapes to represent the key element that you will see on the screen in their simplest form. And they are usually in black and white, and sometimes gray.

The important thing about wireframes is to keep it simple; more detail can be distracting and it is important to keep things to their most basic, fundamental forms.

Once you have gotten some initial ideas down on paper, you might notice that not everything fits quite as you imagined. Take the time to do a quick second sketch and refine key elements if they don't fit quite right. Digital wireframes are a great step after hand-drawn sketches because they are easy to share with colleagues and the rest of the design team, who can continue to add layers of complexity and polish.

Low and High Fidelity Wireframe

UX design fidelity is the degree to which a design closely resembles the visual appearance, feel, and functionality of the finished product—be it a web or app design. The composition of the design, the material it contains, and its degree of utility are the main factors that establish the degree of faithfulness.

Simply put, a low-fidelity wireframe represents the anticipated user journey and layout of a product. A high-fidelity design, on the other hand, will resemble the finished product as closely as feasible within the constraints of the UX design tool being used.

Low Fidelity wireframe: The most fundamental type of wireframe is a low fidelity wireframe, sometimes known as a lo fi wireframe. Its purpose is to depict the general layout of a web page, application, or user interface. Low-fidelity wire-frames aid in communicating a product's main concept and value proposition while excluding finer features like graphics and editorial content. Low-fidelity wireframes usually consist of a grayscale schematic or design that highlights the essential functionalities of an application or website.

Low fidelity wireframes are ideal for early stage design brainstorming and concept sharing because they are quick and simple to develop. The process of developing wireframes also has a very low entrance barrier, so practically anyone can do it. You can even sketch your wireframes by hand if you truly want to take things back to basics. The best thing about low-fidelity wireframes is how quickly they can be created. If you are an entrepreneur with a brilliant idea for a product or service, you may work quickly with your team to develop the most viable solution and then iterate on it.

High Fidelity wireframe: A high fidelity wireframe, also known as a hi fi wireframe, shows how a website or app will appear to the user when held in their hands. In order to accurately depict how a product will look, high fidelity wireframes contain all of the material, stylistic components, editorial copy, and branding that the final product will have. This degree of fidelity allows us to refer to the design as a high fidelity wireframe, but at this stage, you are really working with a digital product mockup. Once you add functioning user journeys and clickable elements to your hi fi wireframes, you have created a functional prototype. These terminologies can often cause confusion in design conversations, particularly when there isn't a professional designer on the team.

After the low fidelity structure of your app or website is established, you can enhance the content and integrate all of your user flows to make your design come to life and convert it into a high fidelity wireframe. High-fidelity wireframes resemble your finished product, making them ideal for early-stage testing. Utilizing wireframing tools such as Figma, you can effortlessly distribute your functional designs to both internal and external stakeholders, along with real customers, to obtain insightful input on your proposed product. The advantage lies in the fact that you can make adjustments based on these comments before constructing a prototype of your ultimate product.

To make things simple, we've described the key differences between low-fi and high-fi wire framing in the table below.

	Low Fidelity Design	**High Fidelity Design**
Structure (screens, Navigational elements)	Core landing pages are included (such as product pages, service pages, and a home page). Low-fi wireframe designs have minimum on-page features to express design purpose (e.g., navigation, core CTAs).	All screens and on-page features are provided to demonstrate the design's full extent and function. Hi fi wireframe designs successfully simulate the final product's appearance, allowing for testing and tweaking.
Content (text, imagery, branding elements)	Low fi wireframe design mockups contain little to no content and tend to be presented in greyscale. Instead of actual assets, low fidelity designs contain placeholder text and imagery.	High-fidelity wireframe designs include all of the final product's images, editorial content, and branding elements. This will comprise headlines, product content, call-to-action buttons, and so on.

| **Inter-activity** (fillable forms and clickable links) | Designs created with low fidelity wireframes are completely nonfunctional. Alternatively, low-fidelity wireframes could have parts of a flow chart to show user flows (a wire flow). | Fully working high fidelity wireframes are the norm, though there are notable exceptions. A user can interact and click links in a high-fidelity wireframe as if they were using the actual product. |

Building a Wireframe

Before you start designing your wireframes, get inspired. Take a look at some examples of wireframes for a similar product to the one you are designing. Most decent portfolios will contain wireframes. So browse through sites like Dribble and Behance to see what other designers have done. You don't need to spend ages on this; it's just a nice way to get into the groove and start generating ideas.

- Afterward, you will need to create the building blocks of your wire frame. It is always recommended that you start with a hand-drawn wireframe. At this stage, you need to be asking the following questions:
- What are the intended user and business goals when interacting with this page? In other words, what does the user want to achieve, and what actions does the business want the user to complete? This could be something like adding an item to a shopping cart, for example.

- How can I organize the content to support these goals?
- Which information should be more prominent?
- What button or touchpoint does the user need in order to complete the desired actions?

All of these, in turn, will get you thinking about where your main message and logo should go and what the user should see first when they land on the page. You will also need to consider where to place your call-to-action. And finally, to think about user expectations—what does the user expect to see at certain areas of the page? Remember, right now, you are just drawing out the building blocks—the bare bones—so keep it simple.

Once you have the foundations in place, it is time to fill in the details. It is advisable to work from top to bottom, then left to right. To determine the kind of details you need to fill in, you need to define usability conventions, such as putting the navigation at the top next to your logo and maybe placing the search box in the top right corner, for example. You will also need to think about spacing, layout, and information hierarchy:

- o What information is most and least important?
- o What is your call-to-action?

Next, think about what images you want to include, where you want to include them, and what size they should be.

All through your wire framing process, there are three big boxes you should be looking to tick – Clarity, User Confidence and Simplicity.

Clarity implies that your wireframe needs to make it clear as to what the page is depicting and what the user can do. Does the layout of the page satisfy user needs? Can the user easily complete their desired actions without too much thought?

User confidence, on the other hand, is all about building trust in your brand through good design. You might wonder what this has to do with wire framing. Well, ease of navigation and clear calls-to-action ensure the product interface is predictable and comfortable. If your page is unpredictable, with buttons and boxes in unexpected places, user confidence will rapidly sink. When creating your wireframe, use familiar navigational processes, place buttons, and commonly use intuitive positions.

Simplicity is all about keeping out the noise. When creating your wireframes, avoid information overload. Excessive contents, links, and buttons can be really overwhelming and distracting for the user, ultimately making it difficult for them to achieve their goals. The user journey should be as smooth and seamless as possible. So, think deeply about what needs to be included on each screen.

Remember, wireframes are not about pretty colors and aesthetics; they are about intuitive and logical layout coupled with good information hierarchy. Also, before converting your hand-drawn wireframes into digital format, you might wish to get feedback on your work so far. If you have the time and resources, consider conducting some quick usability tests to highlight any big flaws that you might have missed.

Clickable Wireframes

Creating wireframes of a mobile screen (Instagram)

First, you need to define elements (rectangle, crossed rectangle, circle, and lines). A rectangle is a very basic object that can be used to represent content groups or functional elements like buttons. The next shape will be a rectangle with a crossed line. The crossed line is used to represent the imagery. Next is a perfect ellipse circle. Circles are used to represent objects like an icon or functional elements like an avatar. Lastly, there is the combination of lines which is used as a textbox placeholder. Place all the shapes into a frame, and align the frame's vertical center.

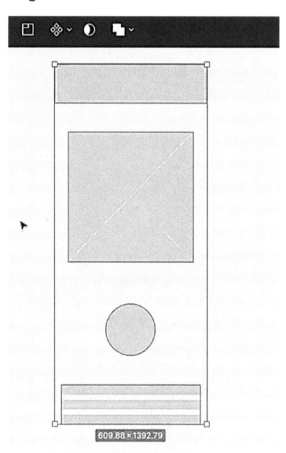

Next, we will need to create a layout for the design. When creating mobile screens, it is recommended to use the size of the actual viewport you are designing for. For instance, if you are designing for an iPhone, you will need to use the size of a viewport port for the particular iPhone.

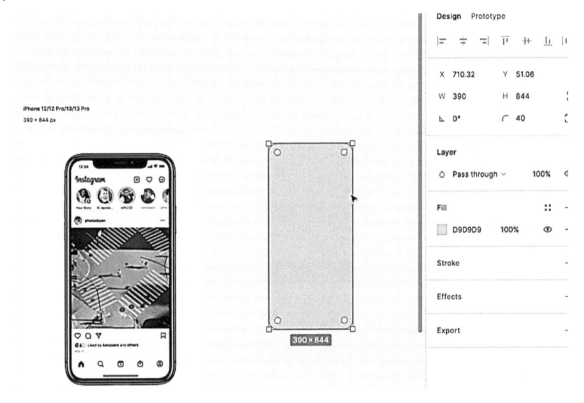

Turn it into a frame and name the frame. Now, let's copy the shapes from the first frame to the mobile frame.

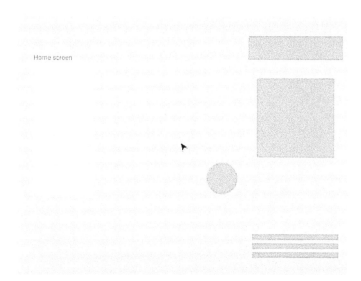

Then, scale it down to fit the screen you are using. Ensure everything you are bringing in belongs to the frame. In other words, make it a child in the parent frame you are bringing it into.

Next, is to bring in functional elements (which are the rectangles) and scale the size to fit, then add contrasting elements by giving some attention to color.

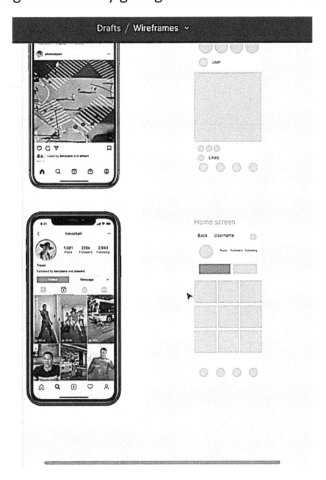

Also, you don't need to be really focused on creating an exact design, because the idea of a wireframe is to give a general idea of what the screen will be all about. So, it is fine when the size over the element is not exact.

Lastly, ensure you confirm from the layer's menu that there is no floating element anywhere and that all elements belong to their frames. To connect these frames together, let's go over to the Prototype. Then, choose the object that will act as an interactive element for the design, and simply create a transition between the two frames of screens so that once the user clicks the object, they can navigate from one screen to the other.

To do that, click the prototype panel on the right sidebar, then click an element on one of the frames, then draw the transition arrow to another frame and back.

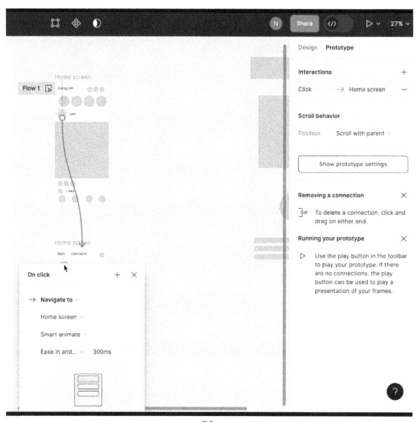

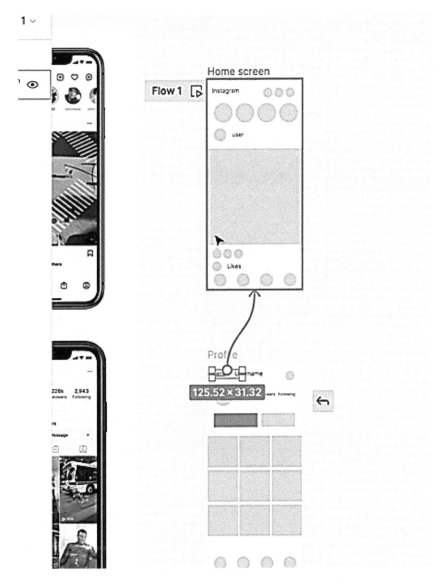

Now, click on the presentation play button at the top right corner of your screen to preview how it works.

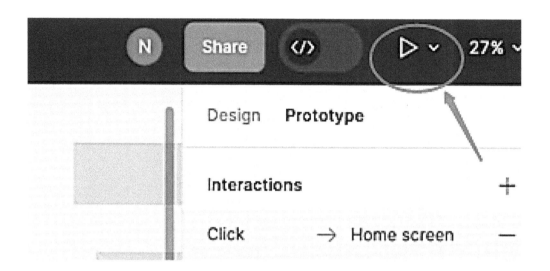

CHAPTER FOUR
AUTO LAYOUT AND CONSTRAINT

Auto Layout and Constraints are two powerful tools in Figma that enable you to automate different scaling behaviors. Although they both aim to reduce manual resizing, their methods of operation differ. Whereas auto layout gives you control over how frames react to changing objects, constraints let you manage how objects react to changing frames.

To put simply, Autolayout is a property you put on a frame to tell the frame's children (element within the frame) how they should act. The frame is therefore considered the parent and any element inside of it is the child. Auto layout as the name suggests, makes the work of laying out elements in your designs automatic. Auto layout can be added to frames to create dynamic frames and components that respond to the size of their child objects, such as a button that grows with the length it labels. You can tell an item to take up all of the empty space available to you and fill their parent container. Use properties like padding to let your items breathe, alignment to change their position within the autolayout frame, or evenly distribute empty space between them.

Auto layout can be applied to almost every one of your components to make them more flexible and dynamic.

Adding Basic Auto Layout

To create an auto layout button, select the text tool, click on the canvas to create a text layer, and type Button for the label. You can add text styles from the panel on the left side of the screen.

With the layer of text selected, use the shortcut **Shift + A** to add auto layout. This places the label into an auto layout frame, which you can add a fill to.

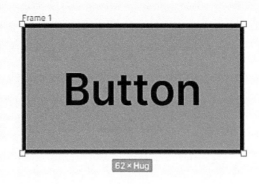

Auto Layout Properties

When you change the label, the frame will dynamically resize to fit. Auto layout frames have additional properties in the auto layout section of the right side panel.

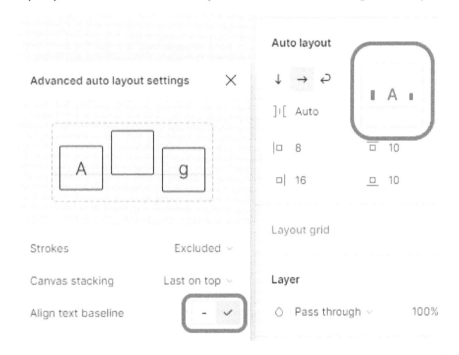

Layout

Auto layout frames can have three layouts, vertical, horizontal, and wrap. Whichever direction you choose will determine the mode of operation that the items within the frame will follow. For instance, in the image below, the item with 'C' has been selected in the vertical frame; duplicating it will cause the duplicate to go vertical too.

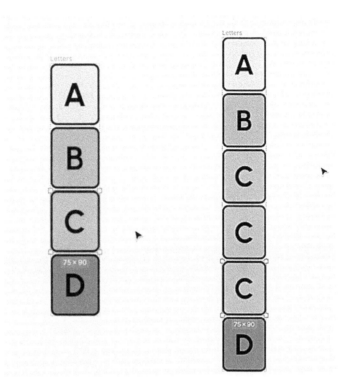

The wrap layout is a hybrid of the vertical and horizontal layouts. As long as you have space for them to be vertical next to each other, they remain on a straight line. However, if the space gets smaller, it drops the horizontal feature in the arrangements.

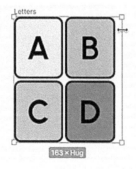

58

Gap/Spacing

The icon with two opposing brackets is known as the gap/ spacing in the auto layout (marked as blue in the first image above). This refers to the spacing between the children inside the auto layout. If you enter 50 as the spacing digit, the items will automatically be spaced out by 50.

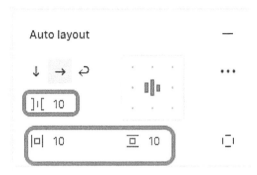

If you make the digit a negative number, like -22, the items will get stacked on top of each other.

With spacing, there are two spacing modes. The mode we just saw above is called *Packed*, meaning manually deciding what the spacing is. However, we can decide to allow Figma to decide for us, which is called Automatic. And there are

three ways of doing this. The first way this can be done is to just type in the word 'Auto' instead of putting a digit. Another way is to select the alignment area and click X on your keyboard. The third option is to tap on the dropdown to reveal the Auto option.

The auto option is very useful because it creates a really dynamic environment such that if the frame becomes larger or smaller, the items will remain evenly distributed, rather than you having to go back and change the spacing.

Padding

Next, you have the horizontal padding and vertical padding (marked as red in the initial image above), which creates empty space between the bounding box of the child items and the bounding box of their containing frame. They are often used to give the item in your auto layout frame some breathing room. You can also enter a number to give the range of padding you want.

The padding field also supports comma separated values that match CSS notation. So, for instance, you can enter '8,16' for the horizontal padding, and it will add 8 points of padding to the right side and 16 points of padding to the left side.

The same can also go for the vertical padding. If you want to control all of the padding at once, horizontal and vertical, all you have to do is hold down *Ctrl* and tap into the padding section. This will cause all of the sides to combine, and then you can type in a particular figure.

▣ 10, 16, 10, 8

Alignment

Still on the auto layout properties panel is the interactive alignment box, which allows you to place the item in specific positions within the frame. However, this is often obvious when the frame is bigger than the items; of course, you can see the items move as you click on different alignments.

Moreover, if you are on packed spacing, you will have nine options on the alignment section, but if you are on automatic spacing, you will only have three option

Advanced settings

By clicking the three dots on the side of the auto layout properties, you get to enter the advanced settings.

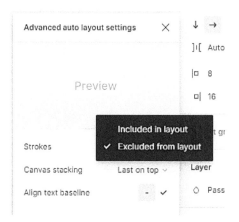

Under Strokes, there is Excluded and Included. Excluded means it is going to ignore the strokes and just look at the element itself and vice versa. The Canvas Stacking option works when there is a negative value for the gap (e.g., -25) and the elements overlap. You can use this option to change which one should overlap.

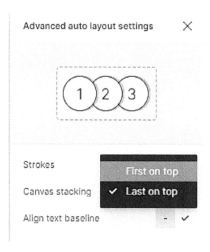

The Align text baseline option, when checked, causes elements such as images and shapes to align with whatever text is on the auto layout frame. And even when new elements are brought into the frame, they automatically adjust the alignment of the text.

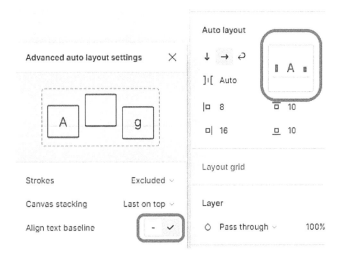

Lastly, one of the cool things about auto layout is that you can move the 'children' inside of the parent frame by clicking the arrow keys on your keyboard.

Resizing Mode

Another intriguing factor in the auto layout is that you can nest them as much as you want, meaning there can be auto layout inside another auto layout.

There are three modes for items inside of an auto layout – Hug, Fix and Fill.

Hug – When a frame is set to the hug content resizing type, it means you don't have control over the size; rather, Figma controls the size of the frame based on the volume of what is in the frame. In other words, the frame 'hugs' whatever size element is in it.

At the same time, you will observe that the manual size control in the Design panel has been grayed out, while the horizontal and vertical resizing options are selected on 'Hug'.

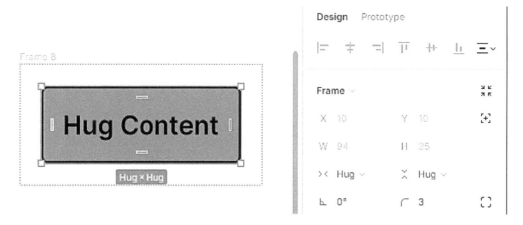

In the image above, there is 10 pixels of padding, which is why the frame is not fully hugging the text itself. If you remove the value of the padding by changing it to zero, here is what you get:

Fix and Fill – A combination of the fix and fill options can give a very controlled outcome.

In the image above, the Width (W) is set to a Fixed width, while the Height (H) is selected to Fill container. However, you would observe some vertical red lines coming out of the diagram when you hovered over the fill container option. This basically means that this element is going to fill up as much space as it can on this axis.

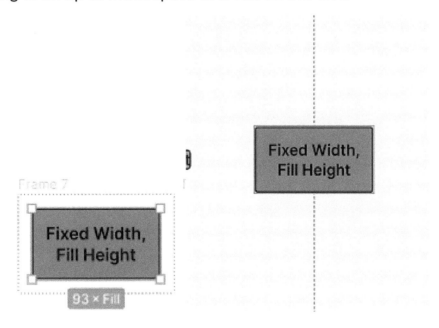

Basically, Figma is giving an indication of what is going to happen, fill basically means that the element is going to fill up as much space as it can on this axis (as long as there is no vertical padding restricting it from the 'parent' frame in which it is situated). So, if the Fill container is clicked, this is the outcome:

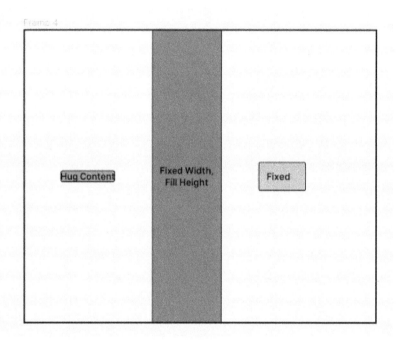

Moreover, the height remains grayed out because Figma is automatically still in control. And if the 'parent' frame shrinks and becomes smaller, the height at which the 'child' frame fills up becomes smaller as well.

The same rule will also apply if we apply the same method to the width instead of the height. However, the only restricting factor for any of the axis not to get totally filled up is the padding, gap and spacing that are operational in the parent frame. Also, when the 'parent' frame is manipulated around, in terms of width and height, whatever is Fixed or selected in Hug remains intact, while the Fill option gets manipulated also.

If you have a multi auto layout with lots of nested auto layouts, there will be some combinations that are not allowed, but Figma will look after that for you and notify you about what has been corrected as well.

Absolute Position

Although we once said auto layout basically tells the 'children' how they should react, that rule is a fixed one. Well, there is one way to break that rule, and that way is known as Absolute Position. The absolute position can be found next to the X and Y sections under the Design panel.

Here is an auto layout that has animal boxes in it. It is set to wrap, which means that if it becomes a bit smaller, some boxes will just wrap underneath.

Putting a crown icon on one of the pictures (e.g the elephant) will cause Figma to see the crown as another auto layout and try to fit it in (thus disrupting the elephant icon).

Therefore, in order to break the rule of the auto layout, we can use the Absolute Position tool. When absolute position is selected on an element, it gets a visual representation of boxy corners around the frame shape (in the layer's) to indicate that it is using absolute position.

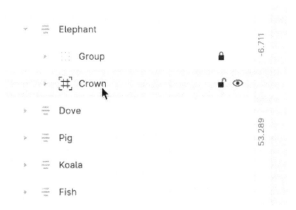

Now, the crown can be moved about on the animal boxes without having to distort it. And even if the shape of the 'parent' auto layout is adjusted and the animal boxes get wrapped, the crown stays with the elephant box.

Finally, keep in mind that if you are using a lot of absolute position, you shouldn't be using an auto layout, because if everything is breaking the rule, then there is no rule. So, just be mindful of the fact that absolute position is not something you should be using frequently; it is there for specific reasons and you should be cautious when using it.

Constraints

With thousands of devices on the market, each with their own screen resolutions and dimensions, designing for each and every one of them will become a never-ending task. Instead, we want our designs to be flexible and responsive, so they can adapt across these screens. Therefore, when designing, frames and objects are often positioned within a top level frame, which are frames that are directly attached to the canvas and represent the screen dimensions of the specific device the design is meant for.

Again, anything positioned within a frame is called the 'child' object and can be constrained to the edges of their containing frame, called the 'parent' frame. Once constrained, they will maintain a set distance or proportion from the parent frame boundaries. Figma displays these constraints as a dashed line extending from the bounding box.

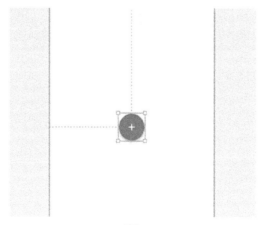

Practice

Create a 300 x 300 square and frame it. Then create a 100 x 100 ellipse inside the 300 x 300 frame.

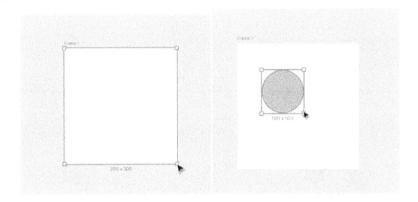

Align the ellipse with the horizontal and vertical centers of the frame.

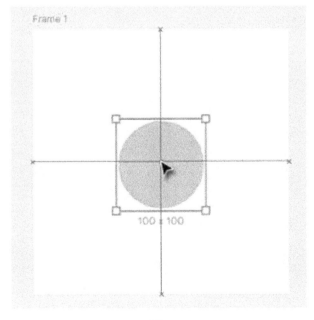

You can set constraints across the horizontal axis to the left, right, left and right, center, or scale. Across the vertical axis, you can constrain top, bottom, top and bottom, center, or scale.

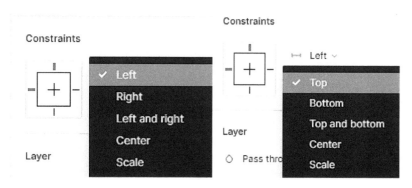

When you create a new object inside a frame, the constraints are set to the top and left by default. Try resizing the frame and see how the ellipse will stay positioned in relation to the top left of the frame.

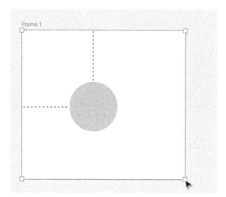

Change the default to the horizontal and vertical centers by selecting the center lines within the constraint box. You can also select the constraints using the menu on the right.

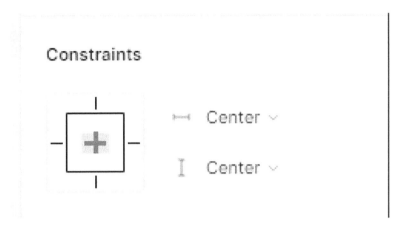

Now, no matter how you resize the frame, the ellipse will remain in the horizontal and vertical centers of the frame.

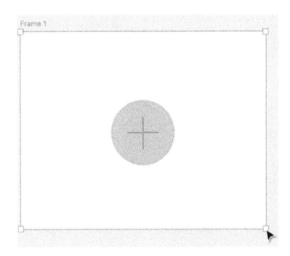

Bringing it to a real world design example, the picture below is of a system bar component for a Google Pixel phone. If the width is resized to fit by dragging the right side of the system bar frame, you will notice that the right side icons do not keep their relative position to the right side of the system bar frame.

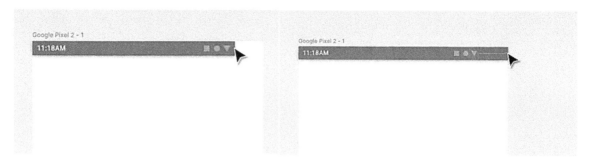

To adjust, press **Ctrl + Z** to undo the resize, then click the component on the right side of the system bar, and then set the horizontal constraints to right, and vertical constraints to center.

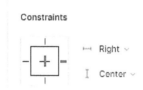

Finally, resize the width to fit the top level frame, and you will see the right side component follow suit.

Layout Grid

Layout grids are visual aids that help you keep elements precisely aligned in your frames. If you are designing for the web, grids can be particularly helpful when thinking about responsive design or how your design will appear on different screens and devices, like a tablet or a laptop. As the window shrinks or grows, a grid can help determine how and which layout adjusts. Layout grids can only be used on frames, which means they can be applied to any top-level frames sized for a device (mobile, tablet, desktop), frames nested within your design, or even frames within your components.

A frame can include as many layout grids as you want. This implies you can combine different grid types on a single frame. Since such grids are applied in the right hand sidebar like other settings, you can also select and paste each one onto other frames. Each grid's appearance (color and opacity) can be adjusted to make it easier to distinguish between them.

Types of Grids

There are three types of grids: grid (uniform grid), column, and row. Uniform grids generate a sequence of equally spaced fields across the frame (like a sheet of grid paper) at the size you specify. The others provide a few extra choices for creating columns and rows. Within column and row grids, you may additionally customize their position and scaling behavior.

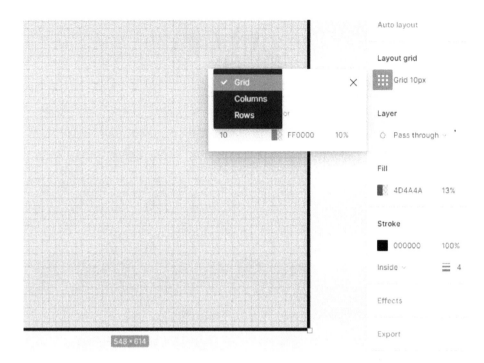

To add a layout grid to a frame, start by selecting or creating a frame within a file. Towards the right, in the middle of the properties panel, is an option to create a layout grid. Click the plus icon. By default, grids that are added to the frame will be a 10 pixel uniform grid, but these settings can be adjusted in the layout grid properties panel, and if you like, you can also adjust the color and the opacity of the grid.

Layout grids are static and pixel fixed, which means that when you resize the frame, your grid remains intact. Figma makes it easy to add multiple grids to your frame. You can add columns, roles, or both, simply select your desired option in the layout grid panel. The Gutter property specifies the space between each column or row, and the Margin property defines the space between the frame and the outermost row or column.

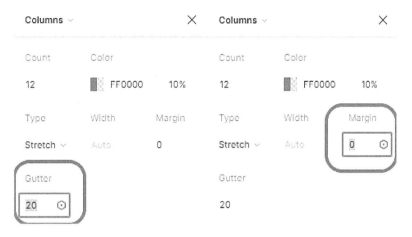

In the second image above, Figma has set the width value to auto, and it is also locked. This is because the layout grid type is *Stretchy*, which means the width of the column will automatically grow or shrink when you resize the frame. If the layout grid type is changed to *Center*, then you can change the width value.

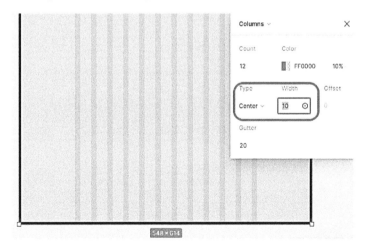

Using a center layout grid can be useful when designing an ultra-wide display, where much of the horizontal space may not be utilized. There are also Left and Right layout grids. This will move the layout grid to the left or rightmost edge of the frame. You can then adjust the offset of the grid to add space before the grid begins.

You can toggle ON/OFF the visibility of the grids in your project by pressing **Ctrl + G** on your keyboard or by clicking the eye icon in the Layout Grids properties.

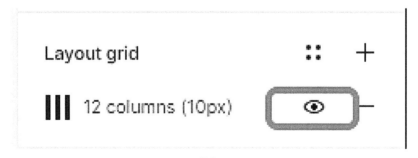

Baseline grids

A baseline grid is created from the baselines on which your typography is based. These serve as visual aids in your design, covering its width and repeating vertically at an even interval. That interval is mostly determined by your typographic scales and line heights. A 4-point baseline is commonly utilized in 8-point grid systems. As you begin to configure different type sizes and line-height combinations, this basic unit simplifies and scales the math.

Using one can help you align one piece of text with another while also providing a unit of measurement to help you determine the sizing and spacing of other elements. The baseline grid is an essential component in many design systems, including Google's Material Design, for determining type size and line-height pairings, as well as margin and padding spacing. If you've ever wanted to construct a baseline grid in Figma, you may do so in a variety of ways utilizing a row grid.

- A grid based on line heights.
- A grid that is formed around the real baseline where the text lies.

Since you have a degree of control over the appearance of the grids, you can design the appropriate grid for either technique. A row grid with the type set to "top" can be used to lay the groundwork for a baseline grid. Usually, it's a good idea to increase the row count to allow for longer scrolling frames. From there, you may emphasize alternate rows or thin lines by combining the height, gutter, and color settings, as shown below.

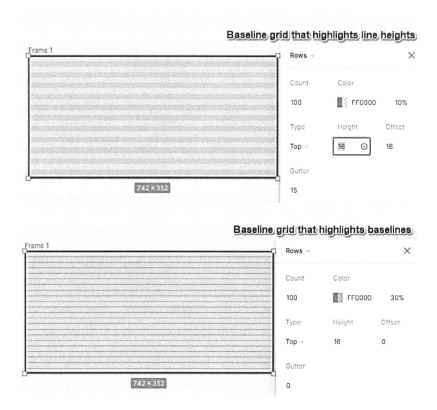

Nested grids

Unlike other programs, Figma does not confine you to a single grid at the "artboard" level. A grid can be applied to any frame; therefore, it can even be applied to frames that are nested within your design. Feel free to go all 'Matryoshka' on your design, creating grids within grids within grids to your heart's delight. Once you've mastered this, there are countless ways to employ grids as visual assistance in specific areas of your design. You may help them stand out by customizing the color and opacity of each grid.

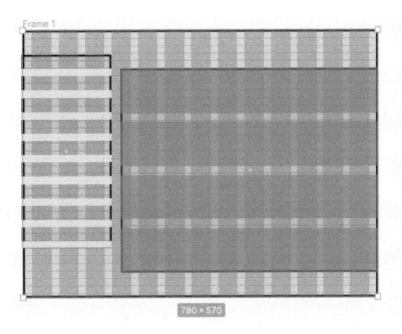

Working with Constraint and Layout Grids

Applying constraints in Figma aids in defining how elements will resize in reference to their parent frame. So, if you want an element to remain pinned to the top right of a frame (such as a close button), using constraints ensures that the element keeps its distance from the top and right without changing size as the frame grows or contracts.

On the other hand, constraints applied to an element inside a frame with a layout grid will be based on the element's closest column rather than the parent frame's borders. When used with stretch grids, this allows your items to remain fixed to columns or rows while leaving a fixed gap (gutter) between them. It results in considerably more realistic scaling behavior.

By properly defining constraints, you may resize things relative to the layout grid, allowing you to keep fixed column gutters and margins. Using the same method, we can add constraints to our earlier example to show nested frames (each with its own grid). This enables you to separately define the scaling behavior of individual portions of your design.

Visualize padding with Grids

Padding is sometimes necessary to guarantee that content remains equidistant from an element's boundaries. You can help with this by configuring a column and row grid with a single row/column, defining the gutters to 0, and setting the margin to your preferred spacing. If your design system includes predefined padding spacing values, you may easily add and apply them to frames or components in your design.

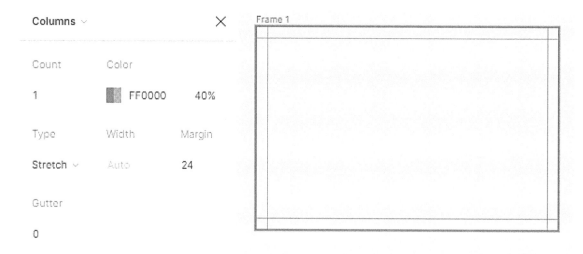

Sharing Grids with Styles

While creating grids, you may wish to experiment with different layouts for different device sizes or other typical use cases. You can combine many grids into a single grid style to make it easier to apply them across frames, files, and projects. That style, along with other styles and components, can subsequently be shared via a team library.

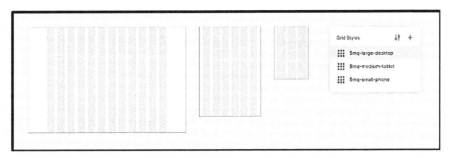

CHAPTER FIVE
STYLING AND FORMATTING

Styles allow you to save certain properties and then later reuse them across your designs, and if you update your styles, the properties will instantly update across the file. Styles can be used to define brand's colors, typography, effect and layout grids. Your color styles can be then applied to fills, strokes, and text in your designs. Your styles can also be published to your team library, and accessed by everyone on your team. You can make Color Styles which can be applied to Fills, Strokes and Text (as a fill). You can also create Text, Effects and Layout Grid styles.

Colors and Gradients

Colors Styles

Start off by drawing a shape, i.e ellipse. By default, your shape fill color will be a neutral gray.

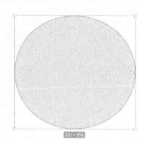

If you look to the Fill section of the properties panel on the right-hand side, you can change this to a custom fill color of your choice by either selecting a particular hue, changing the value, or changing the percent.

Fill

If you plan on using a particular color across your design, it will be smart for you to save this as a color style, so you can manage it and reuse it. Looking back to the Fill section, you can click on the quadruple dot icon to show styles. However, since you haven't saved any styles yet, it would be empty.

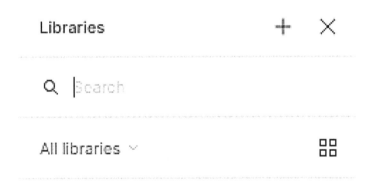

You can create a new color style from your fill color by clicking the plus icon, and giving it a name. Then click *Create Style* to finish up.

The style has now been created and now appears in the styles picker that was previously empty.

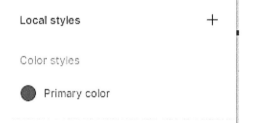

The properties panel also looks a bit different now, where there used to be the custom color picker, there is now the color style. However, it is important to understand that the circle on the canvas is not your style, but a circle object with your color style applied to it. So, if you choose to delete the circle, your style will not be deleted because each style belongs to the file in which it was created as a local style and not to the element in which it was applied. If you want to view your local styles, just click on the canvas to deselect everything, and your local styles will be displayed in the properties panel on the right.

To delete a style, you can right-click it in the list and select delete style. You can also edit a style from here.

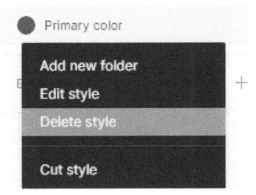

If you click edit style, the pop-up box for style creation will come up. If you change the colors of the style, each element that has the style applied will be updated instantly. Furthermore, let's duplicate the circle to demonstrate a few more things. Now, we have two circles, each with the primary color style applied to them.

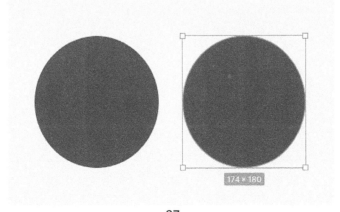

If you hover over the style, a new option will appear – *Detach style*. If you have a shape with the style applied to it and you would rather use the custom color picker, you can select detach style to remove the style. Now, if you were to change the hue of your style, the detached circle would no longer be affected by that change.

When working, it is not required to create all of your color styles right before working. Your color styles are not only limited to being used as fills; you can also use them for strokes. If you create a new rectangle shape, you can go to the Stroke section just below your fill section, click the quadruple dot icon to open the style picker, and the color styles already created in the file are ready to be used.

Styles can also be applied to typography; the image below contains seven different text elements that would be turned into text styles.

Text styles are created in the same way as colors. By clicking the styles icon., then the plus icon, give it a name and save it as a style. With the creation of text styles, you will be able to apply them to text or even substrings of a single text element. Among the various kinds of styles that you can create are Effect styles and Layout Grid styles.

Gradients

Gradients are paints composed of two or more position dependent colors with a smooth blending transition in between. Like solid colors, you can use gradients as paints for fills and strokes on layers or objects. Gradients are utilized in design to give it a sleek, modern appearance. Many brands incorporate gradients into their logos to offer their company and logo a distinctive character that aids in self-promotion. Gradients are a great way to add flair to any design.

Types of Gradients

- ○ *Linear Gradient* – These are colors that align in a straight line. It is the most common type of gradient.
- ○ *Diamond Gradient* – These are colors that originate from a single center point out towards the edges. More like a radial gradient, but with a diamond shape of design in place of the radial's circular fading.
- ○ *Angular Gradient* – These are colors that progress in a clockwise direction from a single point (360 degrees).
- ○ *Radial Gradient* – These are colors that originate from a single center point out towards the edges.

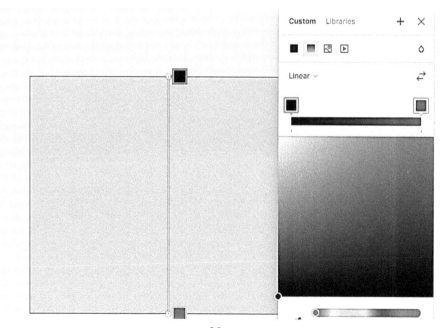

Adding Gradient in Figma

Select the particular layer to which you wish to apply gradient. Next, navigate to the fill and stroke option within the properties panel, and give the layer a particular solid color. Then change your fill from a solid color to a linear gradient.

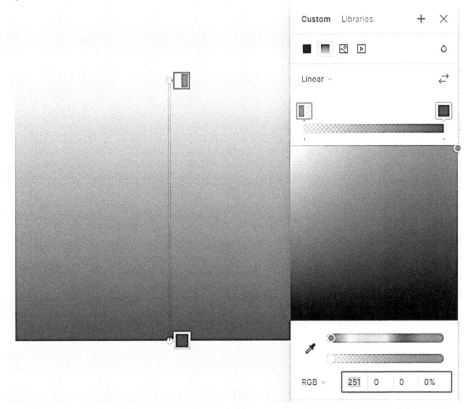

The boxes attached to the line are the different color points of the linear gradient. Dragging the boxes along the line will tweak the fadedness of the color. You can also add more colors to your gradient by clicking on the gradient line in the panel.

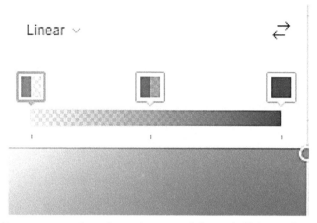

The angle of the gradient can also be changed by shifting the gradient line on your element. Simply click on the white dot and move them around.

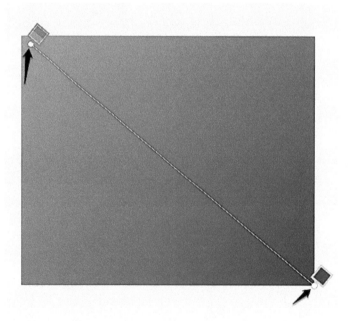

The panel also provides you with options to change the colors as well as the opacity.

RGB ∨ 208 30 30 54%

To change from a linear to a radial gradient, simply go to the dropdown in the panel and click on Radial. Now, you will realize that the white part of the design is centered and moves outward into the red.

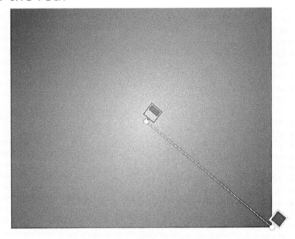

Click on the dropdown to change to Angular. An angular gradient has a fade that goes 360 degrees. You can add more points as well as colors. You can also grab one of the white dots and change the angle while also tweaking the size.

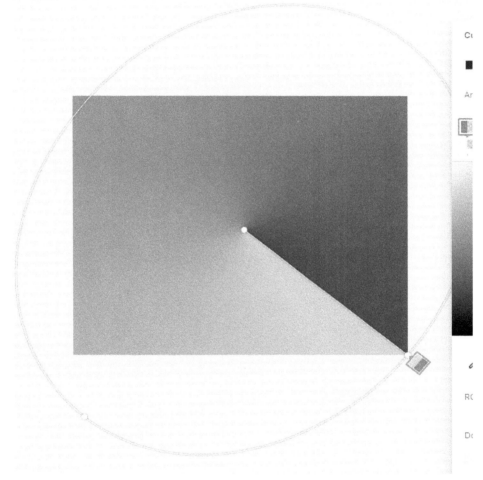

Click again to switch to the diamond gradient, which is one gradient that is similar to radial but with its own unique star-like shape.

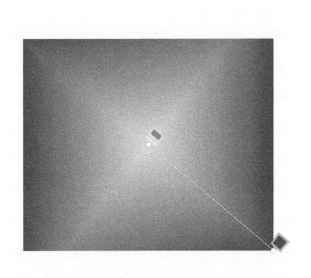

Mesh Gradient

First, create a frame and add a number of different shapes to it. These shapes could be regular circles, rectangles, stars, or even custom shapes created with a pencil.

The more shapes you add and the more you make them different, the more interesting your mesh shapes could look like in the end. Now, you will need to fill your shapes up with different saturated colors.

Next, you would need to add a very high amount of blur to soften the edges and create a smooth transition between these different colors and shapes. So, select all the shapes in the frames, go to the *Effect* tab, and select *Layer Blur* from the dropdown. Next, increase the value of your layer blur to see that the mesh gradient is already taking shape.

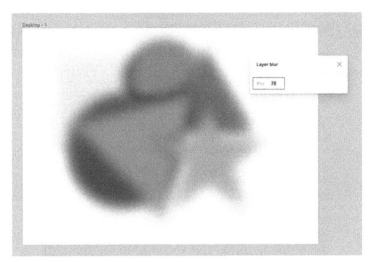

Now, you can go into your shapes, change their size and maybe rotate them a little bit. While also playing around with the different colors to see if you can find something more suitable.

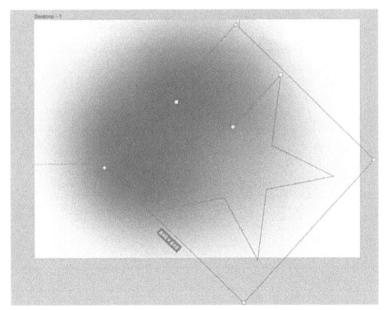

Also, you can change the opacity of those shapes by just clicking numbers on your keyboard. Afterwards, you can select all the shapes and use the Flatten Selection option at the top center of the canvas to merge all the shapes together.

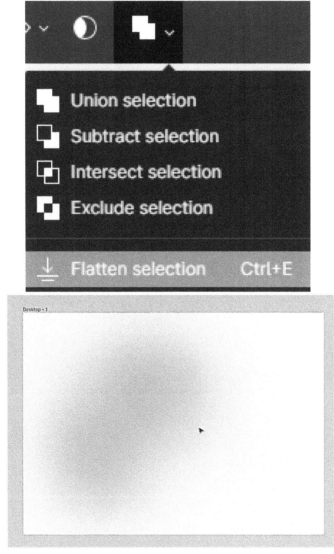

Color Picker

When working inside a file, you will find all of the tools related to color on the right side inside the properties panel. This will be shown once a layer or object is selected.

The eyedropper tool (as indicated in the image above) is used to sample a color, usually from an image, so that you can use the color within the project you are working on. Below is an image with a bright paint color that would be used for a button project.

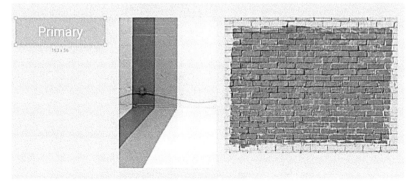

To sample the color and apply it to the button project, one will first start by selecting the button shape itself. This will let the eyedropper tool know that any color that is sampled should be applied to this selected layer. Now with the shape selected, you can click on the Fill tool and select the eyedropper tool, or do a **Ctrl + C**, hover over a desired layer, and click to apply it to the button.

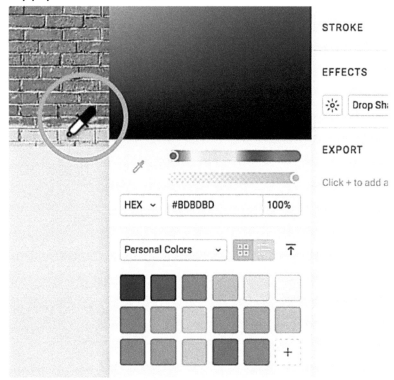

If the color is one you believe you will be using often for projects, you can choose to save it. Simply select the layer that has the color you want to save, click into the color picker tool, and click the plus icon (as shown in the image above). To remove the color, simply right-click and press delete.

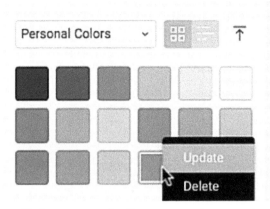

Adding colors to the Team Colors panel allows you to create and share colors with any of your team collaborators. This allows for brand colors to be used and shared seamlessly with teammates to ensure consistency across all designs. If a color is added or updated, it allows everyone to stay in sync with the changes.

When adding and modifying colors in the color tool, you may have seen text fields for both HEX and RGB. A HEX, which stands for hexadecimal, is a six-digit combination of numbers and letters defined by its specific mix of red, green, and blue. A color expressed in hex is most useful in web design and allows for the specific color to be easily taken from Figma, right into code. RGBA, which is an abbreviation for red, green, blue, and alpha, represents the specific combination for each of the three codes to be used on the screen. The Alpha channel in RGBA simply determines the level of opacity applied to the color.

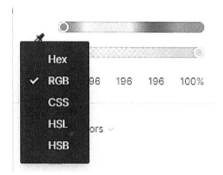

You may have noticed that within the color picker tool, there is a dropdown that allows you to choose between document, personal, and team colors.

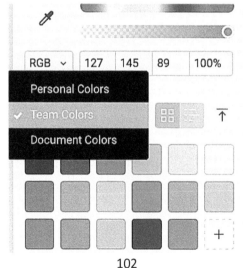

Personal colors are not shared with the team, nor are they document specific. Adding colors to the personal colors panel allows you to use these colors in any project you find yourself in and enables you to save and reuse these colors easily for multiple projects. Adding colors to the document color panel allows colors to be used throughout the document that you are working on. This can be especially helpful if you find yourselves working on a single project for a specific client.

Typography

Text is one of the most important elements in interface design. It can influence your design's legibility and appeal. Your text-related decisions can have an impact on how effectively you communicate your message. Everything matters, from text placement and organization to font selection.

Text tools and Fonts

Fonts are a critical component of interface design, and the font you select determines the readability and appeal of your text; the color, size, spacing, and width all convey a message to the user of your product. Figma comes preloaded with hundreds of Google fonts, so you can start designing quickly. Visit font.google.com to learn more about your favorite fonts, preview a font family or font style, or discover new fonts with various filters.

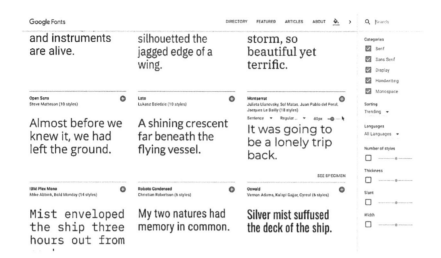

You can also use your local fonts, as long as you are using Figma on a Windows or Mac computer. If you are using the Figma desktop app, your local fonts will be ready to go; no font helper is required. If you choose to use your own local fonts when collaborating with others, each editor will need their own copy of that font in order to edit text using that font.

The text tool can be accessed by clicking the [T] icon in the toolbar or by using the **T** keyboard shortcut.

There are two ways to create a text element, single click and start typing. By default, this creates a text box with the auto resize attribute set to width. This allows the width of the textbox to grow along with your text. Another option is to click and drag to create a textbox with specific dimensions. Since we are determining the size of the textbox in this scenario, the auto resize is set to fix.   This allows longer strings of text to wrap around to the next line once they reach the edge of the fixed textbox you created. It is extending below the bounding box; the box will not resize vertically.

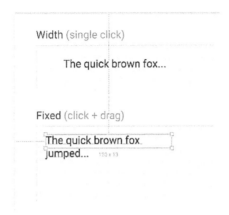

To edit an existing text element, double click inside the textbox.

The text section of the properties panel consists of functions and options to edit your text. First, there is a dropdown menu where you can select a new font, you can also type in the field to search.

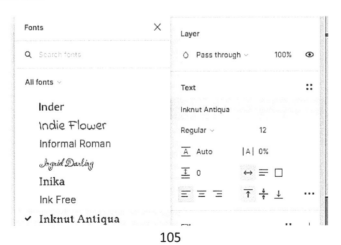

Below are two additional fields, change the font size, view, and select the font styles available for our selected font. Font styles can also be changed through common keyboard shortcuts.

Next is line height, which changes the amount of space between each line of your text. The default value is usually set to auto, which is 100 percent and therefore equal to the default line height for the selected font.

By holding **Shift + ↑,** you can increase it by an increment of 10. To the right of line height is the option for letter spacing, which changes the space between characters.

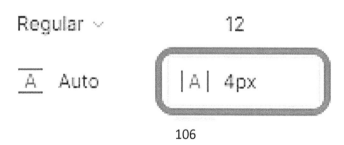

If you would like to adjust the kerning of certain character combinations, you can also use letter spacing. By default, Figma uses percentage values, but if you type in a pixel value, you can change the unit to a pixel.

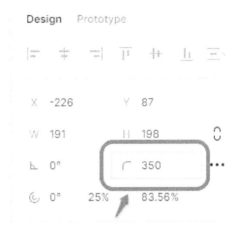

Next, in the properties panel of the text tool, is paragraph spacing. Paragraph spacing changes the space between paragraphs that are separated by returns in the same textbox.

You can also adjust the alignment and the justification of the text to determine where it should be placed within a textbox. The options for horizontal justification are left, center, right, and justified. These options are not only located on the surface of the properties panel but also in the type settings panel within the text section.

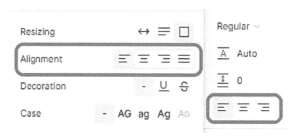

The options for vertically aligning text are top, middle and bottom.

You can also use attributes not within the text section of the properties panel to edit text. For instance, if you want to change the color of your text, add a stroke, or add an effect, you can do that by selecting the text and then editing the fill, stroke, and effect properties.

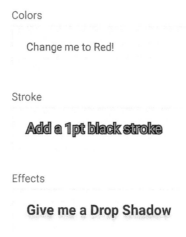

Type settings panel

The Type Settings panel provides access to extra text attributes and OpenType features. Click the three dots in the lower-right corner of the Text section to bring up the type settings window.

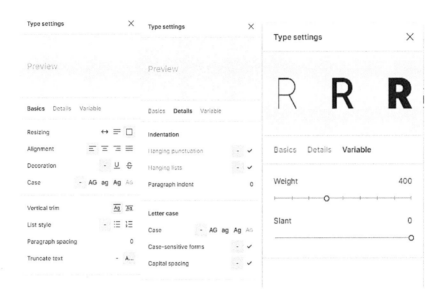

Preview - Use the preview at the top of the type information panel to see how a certain property or OpenType feature appears. Hover over any feature or attribute to see its preview. Figma will offer sample text that is most appropriate for the feature you are previewing. This includes:

- o Text blocks are used to adjust alignment, spacing, and indentation.
- o Numerals represent number attributes.
- o Ligatures or stylistic alternatives impact letters (or letter combinations).

<u>Basics tab</u>

- *Resizing* – select how your text should horizontally resized
- *Alignment* – adjust text horizontally
- *Decoration* – apply decoration (i.e underline and strikethrough) to text
- *Case* – select between lowercase, uppercase, small caps and capitalize
- *Paragraph spacing* – change the spacing between the paragraphs of the text
- *List style* – create bullet or numbered list
- *Truncate text* – truncate text to hide overflow content
- *Max lines* – set max lines to determine when text truncation happens
- *Vertical trim* – toggle vertical trim

Details tab

- *Indentation* – Adjust the indentation settings. Use paragraph indentation to offset the first line of content. You can also choose between hanging quotes and hanging lists.
- *Letter case* – Change the letter case. Choose between uppercase, lowercase, capitalized, and small capitals. You can also change the case-sensitivity and capital spacing if they are available.
- *Numbers* – Apply any number settings, including style, position (superscript and subscript), fractions, and others.
- *Letterforms* – Access all OpenType features, including letter forms, style sets, horizontal spacing, character variants, and more.

Variable tab

Variable fonts allow for multiple font variations in a single file, unlike static fonts, that can only have one. Font authors can customize properties such as weight, width, optical size, and slant to provide additional style options.

Add Emoji

The Emoji can be added to any text layer in Figma, and it uses the Apple emoji style. To add emoji, you must first enable Microsoft's Touch Keyboard.

- Right-click in the Windows taskbar.
- Click the "Show touch keyboard" button.

Now you may add emoji using the touch keyboard.

- Create a text layer.
- Click the Touch Keyboard icon.
- Choose Emoji.
- Choose which emoji you want to use.

Use Spell Check

Spell check allows you to review and rectify spelling problems. Spell check highlights problems with a red squiggly line while in text edit mode, but just for the text layer that is currently active. To get a list of alternative spellings for a misspelled word, right-click on it. To automatically insert the first suggested spelling, click on a misspelled word and then press Tab.

Most people have spell check turned on by default. Spell check is only turned off if your browser's chosen language is not English or Russian and you do not have the Figma font installer installed. Because the Figma online app cannot access the additional languages supported by your operating system without the Figma font installer, spell check is disabled to avoid marking all text in a file as incorrect. Click on the Figma menu. Go to *Text > Spell Check*. Click Check Spelling to enable or disable spell check.

<u>Note</u>: *Spell check preferences set up in the online app are not replicated in the desktop app, and vice versa. When switching between the two apps, you must re-configure your spell check choices.*

Supported Languages

When you use the Figma desktop software, spell check is available in any language supported by your operating system. When you use Figma in the browser, spell check is enabled by default in English (US, CA, UK) and Russian. To use spell check in any other language supported by your operating system, download the Figma font installer. Figma will discover your system's preferred language and utilize it for spell checking. If you are using a Windows device and do not see the language you want to use, you may need to install a language pack. Language packs for Windows.

To modify the language that spell check uses by default:

- Click on the Figma menu.
- Go to *Text > Spell Checker*.
- Choose from the list of available languages.

Add words to dictionary

To avoid spell check flagging words, you can add them to your dictionary. Your vocabulary applies to all files that you can modify. For example, if you add a word to your dictionary in a Figma design file, spell check will recognize the spelling in any subsequent Figma design or FigJam files. Once a term is entered into your dictionary, it cannot be removed.

- o Highlight the term that you wish to add to your dictionary.
- o Right-click and choose Add to dictionary.

Create bulleted and numbered list

Lists are an excellent way to organize and highlight relevant information. Figma allows you to create ordered or unordered lists in the form of numbered or bulleted lists. Figma now supports five levels of indentation.

- Apples
- Bananas
- Oranges
- Grapes
  - Lemons
  - Limes
    - Kiwis

1. Fire
2. Water
3. Grass
4. Electric
   a. Ice
      i. Poison
      ii. Ground

The quickest way to create a list is with keyboard authoring. For bulleted list, you can type in a dash (-) or asterisk (*) and hit Space. For a numbered list, you can type the number and then a period or parenthesis. Also, you can indent up to five levels using Tab or Ctrl on your keyboard. To unindent, **Shift + Tab** or **Ctrl + [**. As you indent, bullets will keep their default styling, while numbered lists will change from numbers to lowercase alphabet to lowercase numerals and then start repeating again.

1. fire
     i. water
        a. gras
2. electric
	• fire
	    • water
	  • grass
	• electric

Also, you can quickly change an individual line from bullets to numbered by typing the (-) and Space or the number and period (.) at the beginning of the line; this will quickly swap it from one to the other.

• 1.fire
1. water
2. grass
3. electric

Keyboard shortcuts can also be used to quickly convert a selection to a numbered or bulleted list. **Ctrl + Shift + 7** will convert to a numbered list, and **Ctrl + Shift + 8** will convert to a bullet list.

• fire
• water
1. grass
2. electric

Convert Text to Vector Paths

Convert whatever text layers you have into vector paths. When you convert text to a vector path, you lose the ability to change the text or any of its related characteristics. However, you will be able to edit the vector pathways when in vector edit mode. This enables you to continue editing text as vector objects, allowing you to:

- o Customize features of a typeface.
- o Create a logo or wordmark.
- o Prepare the assets for printing.
- o Reduce the file / export size.
- o Combine numerous pathways into one item.

There are two ways this can be done: *flatten text* and *outline stroke*

Flatten text – Flattening a text implies that Figma will combine any layers or objects into one and convert editable text layers to vector paths. To flatten a text layer:

- o Select the exact layer(s)
- o Right-click on the layer(s) (either from the layer panel or the canvas)
- o Hit the keyboard shortcut **Ctrl + E** to activate flattening

Double-click on the layer to access edit object mode

A Quick Look at Flattening

Keep in mind that once you have flattened a text, you cannot unflatten it unless you undo the action by pressing **Ctrl + Z**.

Outline stroke – When outlining stroke, Figma converts editable text layers to vector paths, but does not combine any layers or objects into one. To apply this stroke, right-click on the exact layer in the canvas and tap on outline stroke. A keyboard shortcut for this is **Ctrl + Shift + O**. When the Outline stroke is applied, each glyph (or letter) is converted to its own vector node, allowing you to modify each glyph individually.

Images and Mask

Masks are used to reveal specific portions of layers while concealing the rest. They are similar to image fills, but offer added flexibility, such as masking multiple objects and utilizing images with alpha channels or transparency values. This opens the door to using different effects or images with transparent backgrounds as masks, thus allowing for the creation of a wide variety of assets, from avatars to animation.

Creating a simple mask

In the image below, a picture is placed on the canvas, and an ellipse is placed over it. The ellipse is selected, and the Send to Back option is used to place it behind the image. And both the ellipse and the picture are well selected.

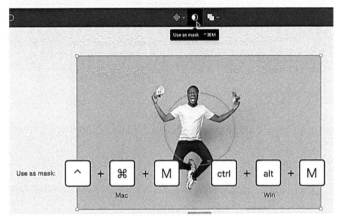

Next, the *Use as Mask* button above the canvas is selected. This creates a mask object inside a group, with the bottom layer acting as the mask and the object it is masking directly above it.

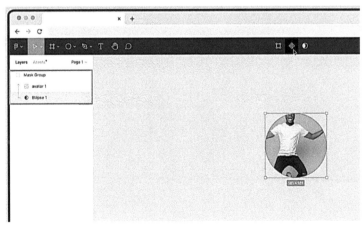

The image and ellipse aren't quite centered, and the image is too large for the mask. The layers of a mask object can be repositioned and resized independently of one another. So therefore, they can be adjusted by clicking and dragging the image and ellipse mask and using the handles of their bounding box to resize.

Text mask

Any object in Figma can be masked or used as a mask, and it is not limited to shapes and images alone. Now, evaluate text as a mask by creating a simple poster. First, create a frame with a fill, add a few vector objects, and include some text.

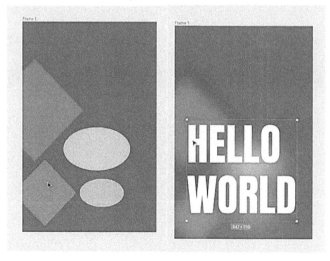

Now, for the text to mask the image, place it behind the image by selecting the text, right-clicking, and tapping on the option *Send to Back*.

Next, select other items and click the mask button in the toolbar or use the keyboard shortcut as indicating in the image below. The result is astonishing.

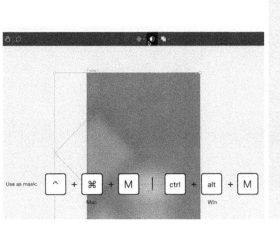

The text mask still acts like a text layer, so you can always change the copy in the future. Doing so will reveal different parts of the object being masked.

Image fill vs mask

When it comes to creating avatars or patterned text, there is the option of using image fills instead of masks. Image fills use fewer layers and you can resize and reposition the image using crop tool.

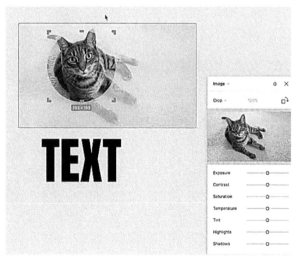

Image fills applied to text also respond when you update the copy. But image fills are mostly great for image objects, while masks are great when more complex designs are required. Particularly when masking more than one object, as demonstrated in the poster illustration, for easy repositioning and resizing the mask, and the object being masked, and for utilizing alpha channels.

Alpha channels

Alpha channels allow you to change the opacity level of an image, object, set of image objects, or set of pixels. If you have used RGBA values in design or code, you may recognize the last letter or position as a transparency value, or alpha channel.

rgba (199, 185, 255, 1.0)
alpha

Because the Figma mask supports alpha channels, you can use images and gifs with transparent background masks, as well as drop shadows and layer blurs. For instance, below is a colorful forest image that will be masked using a portrait image containing a transparent background.

Place the portrait behind the colorful forest image and select both objects.

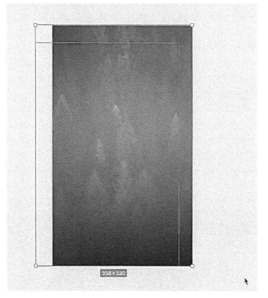

And click the mask icon in the toolbar. The colorful forest image takes shape according to which portions of the portrait image are transparent and which are not, instead of using the outline of the entire image.

Layer blurs and drop shadows

Another channel for using alpha channels for masks is layer blur and drop shadow effects. When applied to masks, these effects behave differently than when applied to layers not being used as masks. For instance, if you apply a drop shadow to a non-mask layer, such as an image, you can update the drop shadow's color independently.

If you apply a drop shadow to a mask, however, the drop shadow also acts as a mask, working to reveal and conceal certain parts of masked objects based on opacity levels.

The higher the opacity, the more the object shows through; the lower the opacity, the less the object shows through; at zero percent opacity, the object won't show through.

Mask and smart animate

Mask objects can be turned into a cool animation. To do that, we will bring the poster example back and make the poster come alive, where the patterns move in and out of the text mask from different directions. First, select the entire frame and duplicate it.

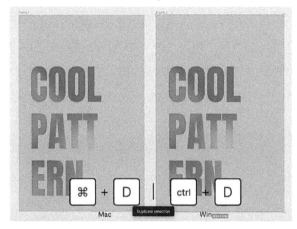

Connect the two frames together in the prototype panel, and set the animation to *Smart animate > Ease in and out back > 1500ms.*

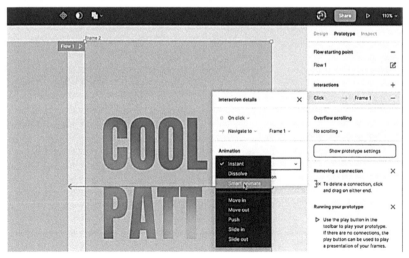

In the original frame, center the text layer vertically and horizontally, and change the frame color to white.

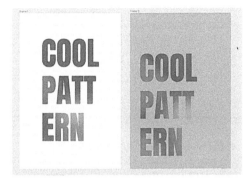

Whether you are creating a marketing asset, prints and animations, masks, and Figma are powerful and flexible tools that expand what is possible for your designs. Alpha channels allow you to use detailed shapes and effects as masks, and combining masks with smart animation can lead to captivating animations for gifs, apps, and more.

Masking is the simplest method for cropping any section of a layer. Using a mask has the primary benefit of being non-destructive; we can choose to always have the masking area visible or invisible. In general, layer masks are a crucial tool for designers using Figma to produce intricate, aesthetically pleasing, and practical designs. Regardless of your degree of experience as a designer, layer masks can elevate your creations.

Placing Images

Images in photography play a big role in visual design. When working with images inside of Figma, it can be helpful to think of them as just a shape with an image as the fill instead of a color.

Start off by drawing some shapes to serve as placeholders for the image you will be bringing.

From here, you can go to *File > Place Image*. However, to speed things up, you can use the shortcut key **Ctrl + Shift + K**.

Then select the images from your system. This will load in the images.

Another way images can be brought into shape after creation is to move over to the properties panel on the right hand side and click the Fill tab. The shape you just created has a solid color fill by default, but you can change this to an image by clicking on the image icon, and a placeholder pattern will appear, and now you can browse for your image.

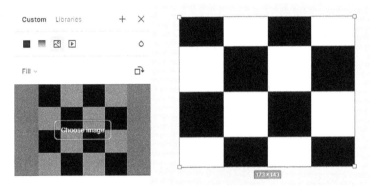

If any image exceeds 4096 pixels in either dimension, Figma may resize the imported image for performance. Once ready, you will see the cursor change to the preview of the image, and you can now click on the shapes to place the images.

If you want to transfer an image to another shape, there is a great shortcut for that – **Ctrl + C** to copy the image, and **Ctrl + V** to paste the image. It's best to think of the image as a fill on the shape and not as its own object.

If you have a component that you want to add an image to, you can hold down **Ctrl** and click on the object inside that component, then use **Ctrl + V** to paste it into that object. If you hold **Alt** or **Option** (in Mac) and double click on an image, you can adjust the cropping.

If you want to change how the image maps inside of its object or reset it back to the filling of the shape, you can change that setting in this property menu. Inside the image drop down menu, the first dropdown determines how the image fills with the shape.

- *Fill* – By default, Fill is chosen. Fill means that the image will fill the container regardless of its size. By increasing or decreasing the size of the shape, you will see that the image responds to the size and fills with the container shape. It is possible to rotate the fill by clicking the icon on the right side.

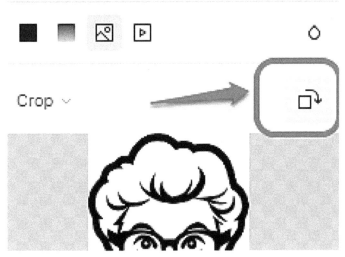

This does not rotate the shape, only the fill.
- *Fit* – This functions similarly to fill, but it may not always fill the entire shape. As the shape is resized, the image will never be cropped or hidden; it will always remain visible.
- *Crop* – This works similarly to most other crop tools that you may be familiar with. As the boundary lines are adjusted, the image inside will always remain the same size. Parts of the image that are outside the boundaries are now faded, and will not be shown once the crop is applied.

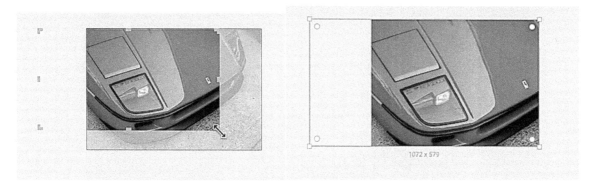

- *Tile* – This function simply repeats the original image as necessary to fill the shape. You can adjust the size using the percent value next to the tile option, which adjusts the size of the tile.

Image adjustment

Image adjustments allow you to make quick but powerful visual adjustments to the image selected using the sliders. You can adjust the exposure, contrast, saturation, temperature, tint, highlights and shadows.

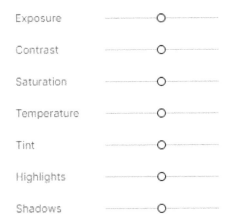

Exposure	―――○―――
Contrast	―――○―――
Saturation	―――○―――
Temperature	―――○―――
Tint	―――○―――
Highlights	―――○―――
Shadows	―――○―――

The edits are non-destructive, meaning they won't overwrite any properties of the original image, allowing you to always revert back to the original.

Vector and Pen tools

Vector graphics are visual, made up of vector points connected by mathematical lines or curves called Paths. Curved paths are controlled by a pair of handles extending from the point called Bezier handles. Unlike bitmaps, JPEGs or PNGs, which will appear pixelated, vector graphics are a lot smaller when scaled up.

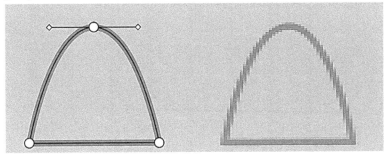

Vector shapes in Figma are handled through a system called vector networks. Vector networks allow you to create lines and curves that connect two or more points. Unlike traditional vector paths, where you need to plot points on a single closed line, a vector network allows you to create complex shapes that are made out of many diverging paths. As you are not limited to one path or direction, you can easily add and remove points in your network and connect them by using two or more paths.

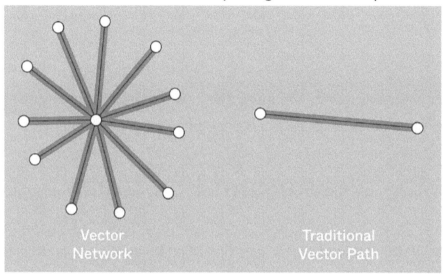

Shape tools such as rectangle, ellipse, and polygon can create basic vector objects, or you can use the pen tool to create and edit vector networks of your own design. With an object selected, click Enter on your keyboard to enter vector edit mode. Once you are in vector edit mode, you can use the Move tool to manipulate each point in the vector network independently. The Bend tool can be used to adjust a vector point or pass Bezier handles to create or adjust curves. Use the paint bucket tool to add or remove a fill to a closed vector path.

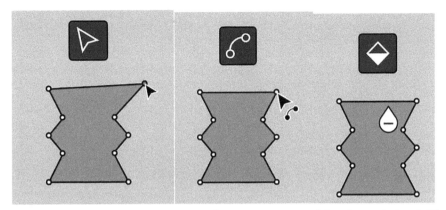

The design panel can be used to apply stroke properties like Cap, Join, Milter Angle, and Dashes to an individual point or to the entire network.

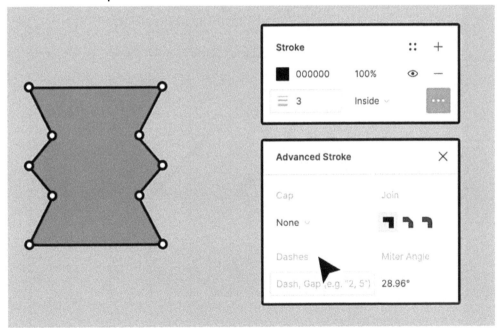

Rounded corners can also be applied to your vector networks.

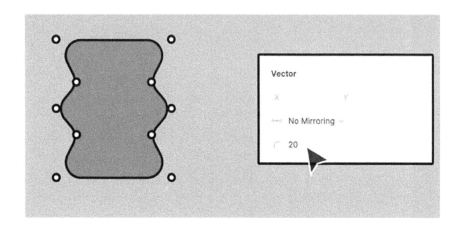

Shape Tool

First, we need to understand how shapes work. One thing to keep in mind with shapes is that when you hover over them, you see extra holes in them, known as *smart shape abilities*, and when you click and drag these holes, the radius is adjusted and the shape is reconstructed.

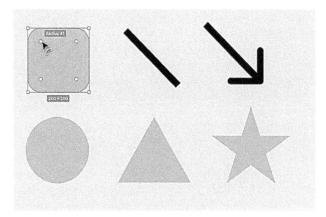

Anytime you select a shape, the properties will be available in the properties panel on the right side.

To get into the vector of a shape, do a **Ctrl + E** to break down the shape, and when you double click on the shapes, you get to see the nodes on that shape, and no longer will you have the ability to use those smart shapes abilities in transforming the shape.

The same goes with text.

Boolean operations

Boolean operations are the composition of multiple shapes. So, all you have to do is overlap two or more shapes on your canvas and select the overlap icon above the canvas, as seen in the image below.

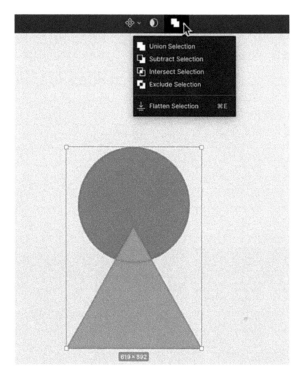

Each one of the options will give you an indicator of what you should expect. *Union* combines the two shape into one. *Subtract* cuts out the overlap of top shape from the bottom shape;

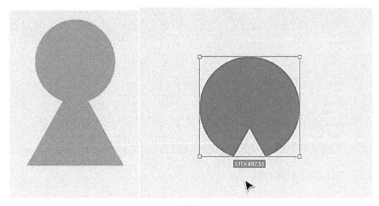

Intersect will actually take out the two shapes and leave the areas they both intersected; *Exclude* does just the opposite of intersect, which is to take out the intersection part and leave the two shapes (while they both adopt the color of the top shape).

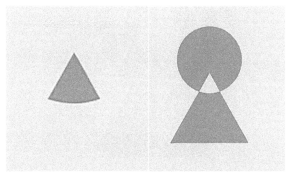

One interesting thing about these four options is that the shapes are still independent of each other in layers (although grouped) and they can be moved individually. This also lets you apply border radius to an entire shape, which makes it unique.

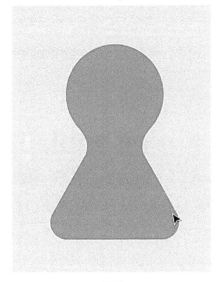

Also, you can still use those Smart Shapes abilities along with the Boolean operation to get a unique combination.

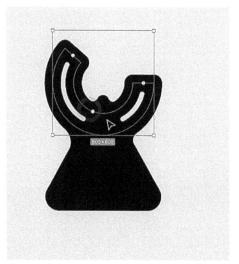

You can also select both objects and flatten them to join both layers. Now, when you hit **Ctrl + E** to break down the object and double click to bring out the nodes, the objects appear as one.

You can play around with the different options and functions to produce more unique results.

Pen tool

To select the pen tool, click on it in the toolbar or hit the keyboard shortcut **P**. Create a vector point by clicking anywhere else on the canvas. Figma will automatically switch into vector edit mode. Click again to create a second point, see how the two points are now connected by a black, one point centered stroke. Holding Shift while moving your pen will snap your cursor to a 45-degree angle. Click and hold to create curved Bezier handles for a point. Once you have created a third point, move your cursor back to the starting point. The pen tool displays a small black circle when closing a vector path.

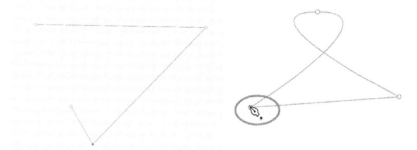

Once a path is close, you can add and remove a fill by using the paint bucket tool found in the toolbar or by tapping the **B** key.

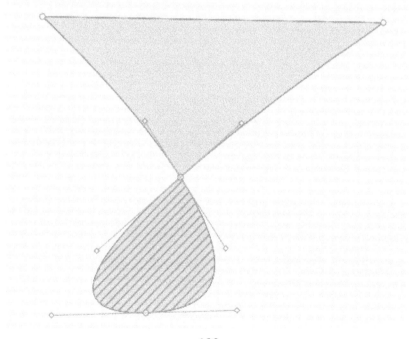

To the left of the paint bucket tool is the bend tool, which changes a point Bezier handles to create a curved line from a point or create and adjust a curved path. When adjusting Bezier handles, use *Alt* or *Option* to turn off mirroring for your point's Bezier handles.

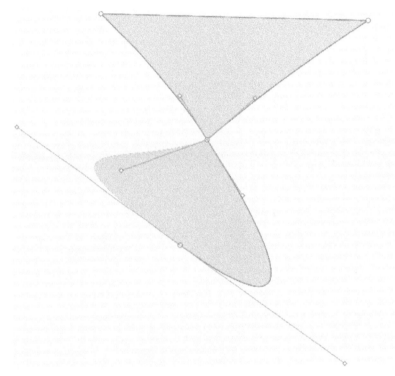

The move tool can be used to select and move a point, path, or group of points or paths within a vector network. For more precise movements, use the arrow key on your keyboard to nudge your selection. After selecting a point or path, you can remove it by pressing Delete or Backspace. Holding Shift and Delete/Backspace while clicking will delete and heal, meaning it will delete the point while retaining the underlying path. To exit vector edit mode, press the Done button, the Return or Enter key, the Esc key, or double click an empty space on the canvas. To enter vector edit mode, press the edit object button, double click on a vector network, or press the Enter or Return key with the layer selected.

Using the pen tool and vector network in Figma, you can create icons, irregular polygons and even complex illustrations.

3D Shapes in Figma

First, you need to create a shape, i.e an eclipse. Then give it a fill or a gradient, if you wish, to make it stand out. Next, take your pen tool and draw out a sequence of lines that would most likely form a 3D shape. Click Done to move out of the pen tool after drawing.

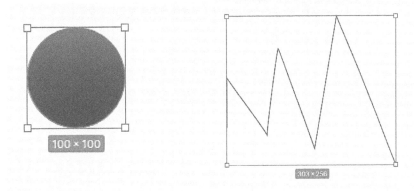

Now, select your line, hold down the Shift key, and tap on your shape wherever it is on your canvas. This will cause the selection to extend towards the shape.

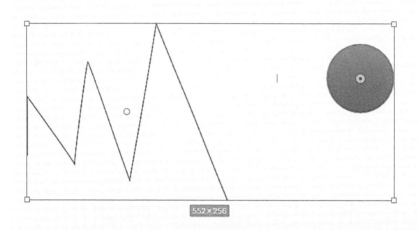

Now, move over to your *Resources* bar above, open it, and click the *Plugins* tab. Click on the search field, type Blend, and click on the one shown in the diagram below.

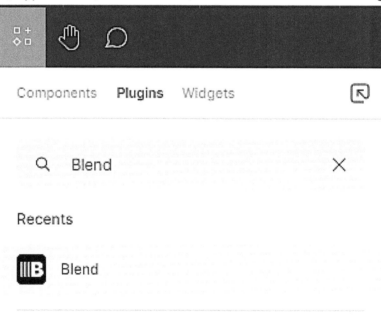

Then hit *Run* to open a constructive dialog box. You can use the values shown in the dialog box below, or you can get creative and make something unique.

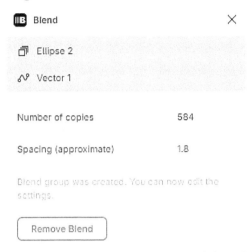

Once the values are inserted, your 3D shape comes to life. Then you can close the dialog box.

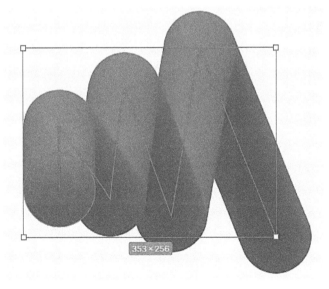

Effects

Effects can be applied to layers and objects to change or adjust their appearance. This can be especially helpful when you are working to improve the appearance or aesthetic of a design.

Shadow

There are two types of shadows that can be used within Figma; Drop Shadow and Inner Shadow.

Drop Shadow: A drop shadow is an effect that casts a shadow below the layer or object to which it is applied. Drop shadows are used to give the impression that the element is raised or floating above the background behind it. And they are often used on buttons, windows, and menus within a design.

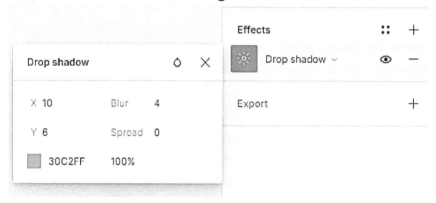

Shadows can be customized to your exact liking by specifying their offset, blur size, softness, color, and blend mode.

The image below is an example of a button, which by itself looks decent, but there is still room to give it a bit more attention through the use of a drop shadow.

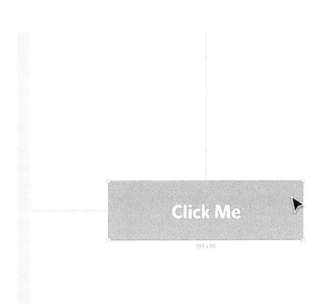

Start by clicking on the shape layer itself. Then, going over to the properties panel on the right, there is a section called effects. Clicking on the plus icon causes Figma to apply a drop shadow by default to the selected layer.

You can then click on the style icon (indicated by the sun) on the left to customize the shadow. The eye icon beside the style refers to the visibility of the shadow. In the style icon, there are a variety of controls that can be used to modify the shadow. Editing a shadow's blur will increase or decrease the size of the shadow. Adjusting the value of the X position enables us to move the shadow on the X or horizontal axis; likewise, adjusting the Y position allows us to move the shadow on the Y or vertical axis. Also, instead of using the default shadow color, which is black, we can use the eye-dropper tool within the color selector to sample the color to be used for a button. The percentage field enables us to edit the opacity of our shadow, while the spread field expands the area covered by the shadow.

145

Click Me

Adding a drop shadow to a button will help it stand out a bit more.

Click Me

Inner Shadow: Inner shadows can be used to apply inner depth to a layer or object. Using the same button as the above illustration, let's see how it might look to have a deeper state. Again, click on your shape layer, then over in the properties panel, click on the Plus icon in the Effect section to create a shadow. then click on the dropdown to select *Inner Shadow*.

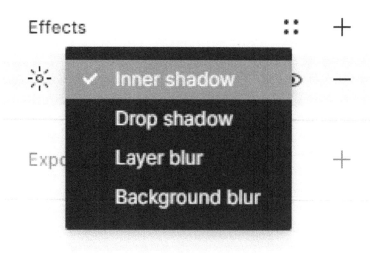

Inner shadows share all of the same controls that drop shadows have, and can be changed in the same way.

Layer Blur: The layer blur effect blurs any object or layer on which it is applied. You can also adjust the blur value to adjust the intensity of the blur.

Background Blur: This would blur any layer or object that is underneath the layer. In the image below, the background behind the image box will be blurred to make the text more legible.

First, start by clicking on the background layer, and then again select effects. Selecting background blur will immediately blur any parts of the image that lie directly behind the shape. Again, the blur value can be adjusted to determine the intensity of the blur.

Two common effects that are not on this list are inner glow and outer glow. However, these effects can be easily created by using an inner shadow or a drop shadow and adjusting our blend mode to screen. Using a light color for the effect color will give us the effect that we are looking for.

CHAPTER SIX
COMPONENT AND VARIABLE

Component properties

Design system builders have different workflows than those who use them. However, both groups want to design systems and components that are easy to understand and use. For instance, if there is a button component in a design system, how would one know what part of the button they are allowed to change? Do these buttons always have to have text? Can the icon be swapped for something different? Design systems often come with documentation that answers these questions. But what if these guidelines can be built directly into the component in Figma.

Variants can be used to define these limits, but as the design system grows, using variants alone for every possible combination can make the design file bloated and harder to manage. With component properties, you can define which part of a component can change. And instead of creating separate variants for buttons with and without an icon and with and without text, you can use component properties on a single variant to toggle them on and off. Thus reducing the number of components needed. This practical takes the guesswork out of designing for anyone using these components, and they can quickly make adjustments as Figma keeps component property controls in one place.

Component properties are properties of your component that allow you to assign names and values within your component that can be customized. There are four different component properties; *the boolean property*, *the text property*, *the swap instance property,* and *variant property*.

Creating Button Component

In this illustration, different types of buttons will be created; with an icon and text, with an icon alone, and a text only button.

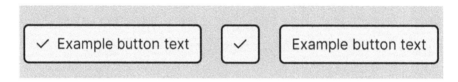

When using this component, we also want to be able to:

- Swap the icon (for a different one)
- Change the string of the text
- Hide or show the icon
- Hide or show the text

To do these, we need three types of component properties; instant swap property, the text property, and the Boolean property.

First, select the button and turn it into a component in order to use a component property.

Mac | Win

Instant Swap – Since we want to be able to swap the icon out for a different one, we would give it an instant swap property. This property is great for showing which child instance you can swap out. Select the icon and go to the right-side properties panel. Next to the instant swap menu, click the component property button.

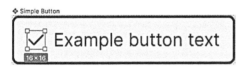

From the modal that will pop up, name the property 'icon' and set the default instance to *Checkmark*. When you are done, click *Create Property*.

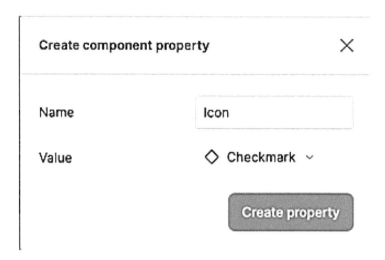

Figma replaces the instant swap menu with a purple component property pill. This shows Figma has created the property and applied it to the selected layer.

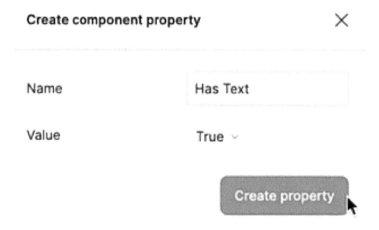

Now, when an instance is created, the component property controls in the right-side bar can be used to swap the icon out directly from the parent component.

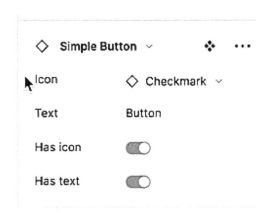

As a note, if the instant swap property wasn't applied to the icon, you could still swap it out for a different one; however, you would need to select the icon instance directly to make this change, as it wouldn't be available in the parent component, property controls.

Text Property – A text property will now be added to show HOW you can edit the button's label. First, select the text layer and go to the content section of the right sidebar. Click the component property button to open the creation modal.

Name the new property 'Text', and the default value 'Button' the click create property.

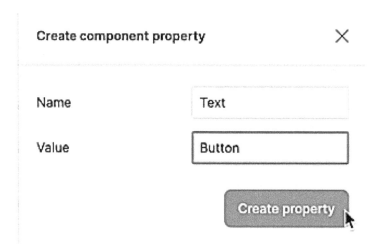

The button text will then change to match the default value that is set. When you then go to edit your instance, you can update the text directly from the right sidebar.

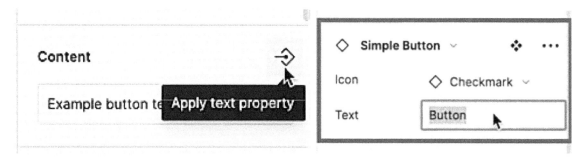

Boolean Property – This provides the option to either show or hide the button icon. Booleans refer to data as having two possible values, e.g., True and False, Yes and No. You can think of a Boolean as a light switch with two possible modes (ON or OFF). In Figma, a Boolean property uses the values *True* or *False*. When this property is applied to the icon's layer visibility, a true value shows the icon, while a false value hides it.

To try it out, select the icon and click the component property button in the layer section of the right sidebar. Rename the property 'Has Icon' and set the default value to True so that the icon is visible. Then click Create Property.

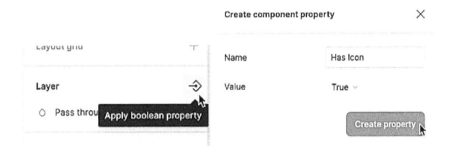

There should also be an ability to hide and show the text, so create a Boolean property for the text layer. Name it 'Has Text' and set the default to True.

Tip – If you ever need to edit component properties after they are created, select the component or component set and use the right sidebar to update their names, reorder the default values, and more.

Now, with our component properties defined, select the instance and check out the right sidebar. You will find all the controls for the component properties that were created in one place.

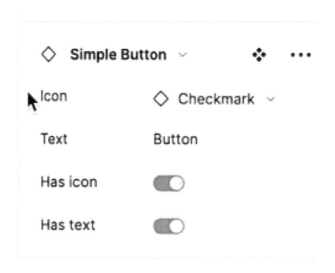

When we use these components, we can stick to the list of controls and not worry about changing other properties. We can then create a variety of buttons by swapping out icons, updating the text, and hiding layers without having to select a child layer.

Variant Properties

Variants are individual components that live inside a component set and carry specific attributes like size, layout, or state changes that are defined by variant properties. Variants are great when you need component variations or when you need to create interactive components.

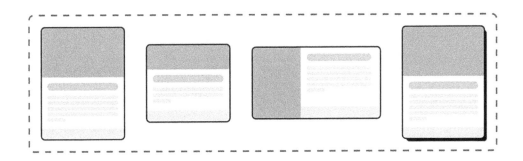

To show how variant properties work, below is a message component. This component appears in a user's inbox and contains a preview of the message, varying information about the sender, and an unread indicator. It already has the Boolean and text properties we need, but we would like to create a new state that shows when a sender is actively typing a message.

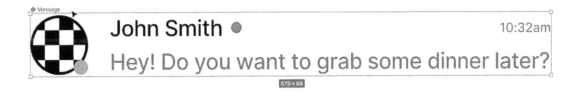

First, select the component and then click *Add variant* in the tool bar just above the canvas. This will duplicate the components, including their properties, and place both components into a component set.

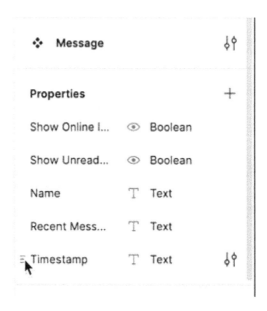

From the right sidebar, you will see that adding a variant also creates a variant property with the name and value. Now, update the variant property by changing the name to State and the value to Typing.

When a new variant was added, Figma also applied the new variant property state to the original component. Select the original component, and you will see the value default next to the state.

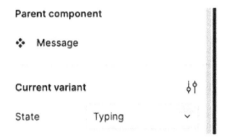

To add more variants to an existing component set, click Add Variant from the toolbar or click the plus icon below the component set. Now, you can edit the new typing variant by changing the message preview to a blue typing label. Select the message preview layer and go to the Content section of the right sidebar. You will see a purple pill for the text properties. The goal is to change the text, but if you try to update it on canvas, it will update the text on the other variant. Instead, hover over the purple pill and click the detach property icon to unlock the property from the text layer.

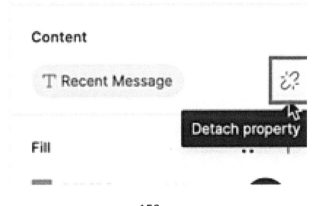

Now, the text can be updated without affecting the other variant. The fill will also be updated to a blue color, and the new variant will be all set.

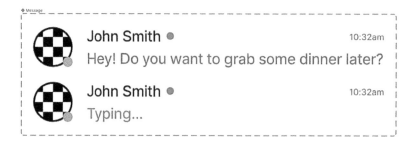

Add Component Properties

So far, the basics of component properties have been well covered. But what if you have a design system that is already in use? Therefore, let's delve into how we can adopt component properties into an existing component set. Below is a button component set with icons on the left having three states; idle, hover, and active, and four types; neutral, positive, destructive, and disabled.

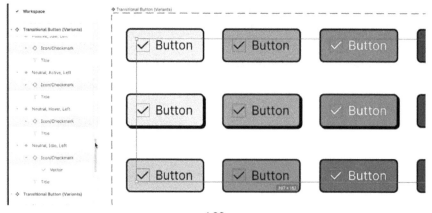

160

Set up the Left Icon

The instant swap properties would be used to swap the left icon for something else, and the Boolean property would be used to show or hide the icon. Select the icons and click the target button below them to select similar layers.

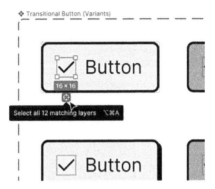

This selects layers from other variants in the component set based on matching hierarchy and layer names. To match, the icons must have a name, forward-slash, 'checkmark', and the direct children of the respective variants.

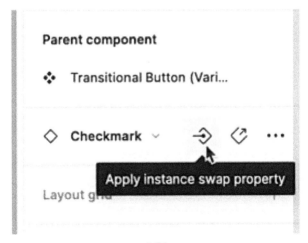

Next, let's create an instant swap property. The name will be set to 'Icon left' and the checkmark instance will be kept as the default value.

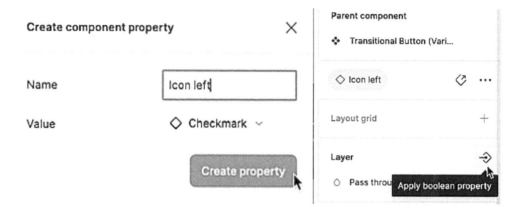

Click create property, and the new property will apply to every selected icon. We would keep the icon selected so that we could add a Boolean property to it. The name will be set to 'Has left icon' and the default value will be set to True to keep the icons visible by default.

Set up the Right Icon

We would need the same property types as the left icon buttons. Keep the icons selected, and Duplicate (**Ctrl + D**) the icons.

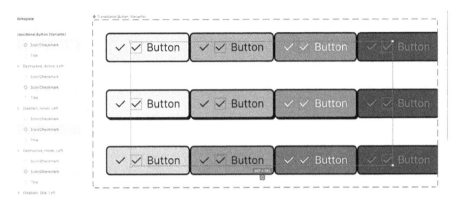

Since the icon is in an auto layout frame, arrow keys can be used to reorder objects in the frame. Hit the right arrow key to move it to the other side of the text.

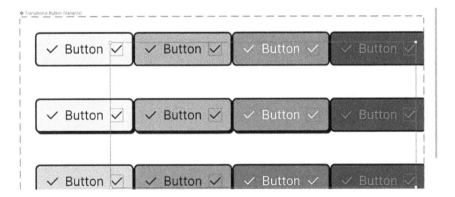

In the right sidebar, you will see that both the instant swap and Boolean properties in the left icon have been carried over to the right icon because they were duplicated.

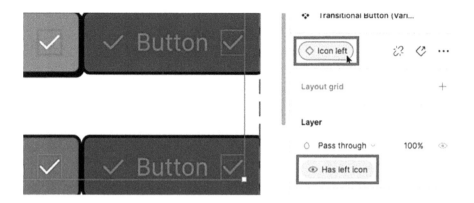

However, this icon needs to be toggled independently. To solve this, the right icons will be given their own properties. Click on the instant swap property to open a dropdown menu, and click *the Create property*. Now, it will be named 'Icon right' and the default value will be kept as Checkmark.

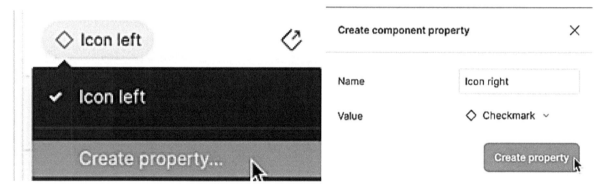

Also, click the existing Boolean property and do the same. But this time, let the default value be set to False to hide the icon.

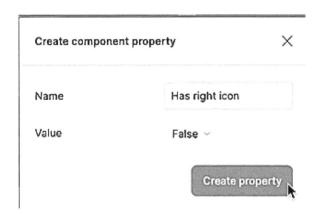

Set up the Text layer

Now, we would need a text property so the text string is changeable and a Boolean property to toggle the text layer visibility on and off. Instead of creating component properties from the text layer, let's create them from the component set. This flow is useful if you need to apply existing properties to a new layer or object. So, select the component set and click the plus icon in the properties panel of the right sidebar. The dropdown menu shows component properties you can create.

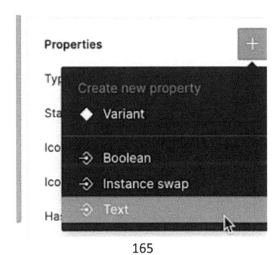

165

Select Text to create a text property, keep the property name as Text, and type Button for the default value. Next, create a Boolean property by going back to the dropdown and selecting Boolean. Name this 'Has text' and set the default value to True.

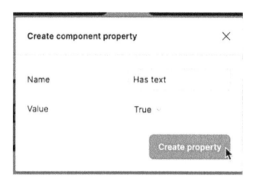

Once the needed properties have been created, they can now be applied to the text layers. Now, select the text layers in the component set by clicking on a text and then the target button to select similar layers.

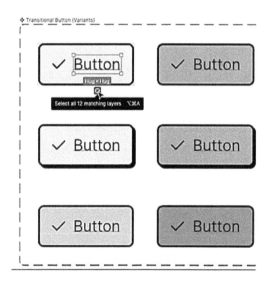

For the Boolean property, go to the Layer's section on your right sidebar and click on the button. Since there is a Boolean property available on this component set, a dropdown menu appears, and instead of going straight to the creation modal, from the menu you can either select an existing property or create a new one. Then select 'Has text; to apply the Boolean property that has just been created.

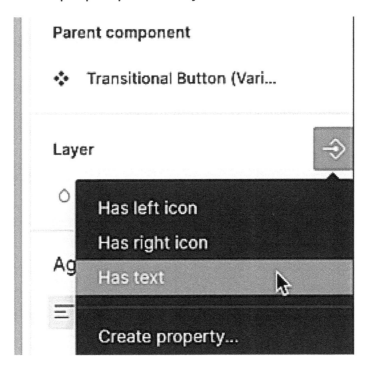

Next, go to the Content section, click the component property button, and select Text to apply the text property that was previously created.

Now, when an instant of the updated component set is created, component properties can be used to make every variant of the original component set.

Click + to replace mixed content.

Also, when using them in a prototyping flow, their interactions work just as expected. The buttons go seamlessly from *Idle* to *Hover* to *Active*.

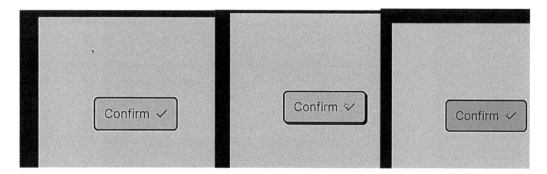

CHAPTER SEVEN
PROTOTYPING AND ANIMATION

An interactive prototype allows you to demonstrate how a design will behave. This is useful for design critiques or for helping others visualize how a design might look and feel once the final product is built. In order to assemble a prototype, there is first a need to have a design built. Designs are created in the *Design* tab, and prototypes are created in the *Prototype* tab. Prototype mode can be accessed by clicking from the *Design* tab to the *Prototype* tab at the top of the properties panel.

This is where you will construct and edit a prototype of your design. The first step in creating a prototype is determining where to start. Below is an example of a thumbnail image for the Great Smoky Mountains National Park in the first frame. We will start by having the image selected. With the image selected, a blue circular node appears on the right side of the element. This indicates where a prototype connection can begin. By clicking on the node and dragging the cursor, a connection arrow appears.

This connection arrow can be dragged to any top-level frame on the page except the element parent frame. When the cursor is released, Figma will create a connection between the thumbnail element and the destination frame. Connections can also be removed by clicking on the connection arrow, dragging it to an empty area on the canvas, and releasing it.

Once you make your first connection, a small blue box with a white arrow will appear on the top left side of the first connected frame. This indicates the starting position of the prototype.

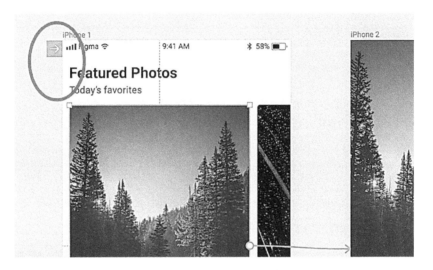

If you want to change the starting frame, simply click and drag the arrow to a new frame.

Presentation View

Once a connection has been created, you can go ahead and click on the presentation view by clicking on the play icon in the upper right corner of the toolbar to see it in action.

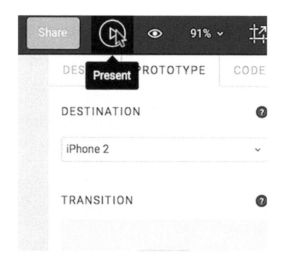

This will open up your prototype in a new browser tab. In the presentation view, you only get to see a single frame in the center of the screen. You can navigate through the frames of your design by using the left and right arrow keys on the keyboard or the arrows icons under the frame. Figma displays each top-level frame sequence in the order in which they appears on the canvas.

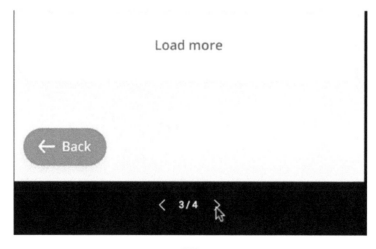

In the prototype, you will notice that if you click outside of the thumbnail image that was connected earlier, a blue bar will flash over the image, this is a visual indicator of a hotspot.

When you click on an area that was not linked to another frame, Figma will show you which hotspots are available. Hotspots are useful when you have multiple elements within a single frame to connect to different top level frames. Therefore, click on the thumbnail hotspot to see how the connection you made plays out.

For a continuous flow of connections, have the last element connected back to the first element to ensure there is no dead end. However, if you want to do it, just ensure that the flow continues any way.

The presentation view has some additional features; on the left side of the toolbar is the option to add comments. In the top right corner is a scaling dropdown menu that defaults to *Actual Size*. Scaling options determine how the design will scale to fit the screen there.

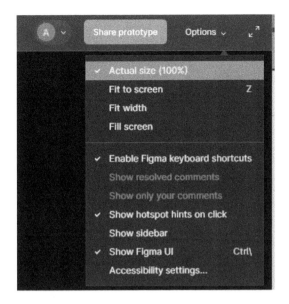

The pixel density of your computer's display and the scale of the operating system or browser can affect the size to which your preview appears. At the bottom right corner of the presentation view is the option to *Restart* the entire presentation.

Prototyping and Transitions

Communication is one of the most important aspects of design. Static designs communicate how your products look, but prototypes let you experience how they might feel. Use prototypes to test and tune your designs, or share them during the user testing study to validate your ideas before investing in development. Prototyping in Figma allows you to build connections between frames, define triggers and actions, and create transitional animations with Easing options to bring your prototype to higher fidelity.

Customizing Prototype Interactions

Prototype interactions and animation can be customized. Selecting a connection will open the interaction details window from the right side panel (or right at the connection spot), where you can customize your interaction. You can view and select the trigger, action, transition, and other properties of the animation, including duration, direction, and Easing.

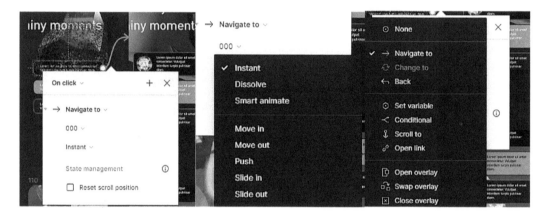

You can also add additional interactions to your connections by clicking on the plus icon in the right side panel. Click the minus icon to remove an interaction.

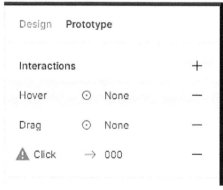

The triggers determine what type of interaction a user needs to take to start a transition. This could be a mouse or touch interaction like tap, drag, click, or hover. The action defines the type of transition that occurs when the trigger criteria are met. The default is set to *Navigate to*, which takes the user from one frame in your prototype to the destination. Other options include *Back*, *Open link*, *Open Overlay,* etc.

After selecting your triggering action, you can select the animation, which defines how the action moves from the starting point to the destination. First, you can choose the transition types; *Instant* immediately takes the user to the destination. *Dissolve* fades in the destination on top of the original frame; *Smart Animate* matches layers between each frame and animates the changes to properties like position scale and color between them. *Move in/Move out* will slide the destination frame into or out of view above the original frame; *Push* will push out the original frame as the destination frame is moved into view. *Slide in/Slide out* will move the destination frame into or out of view as it offsets and dissolves the starting frame.

For Move In/Move Out, Slide In/Slide Out, and Push, you can set directions to left, right, down, and up. You can also Smart animate assets inside those transitions for more detailed animations. All of these animations can be previewed by hovering over the preview window. Except for Instant, all animation options have the ability to control their Easing.

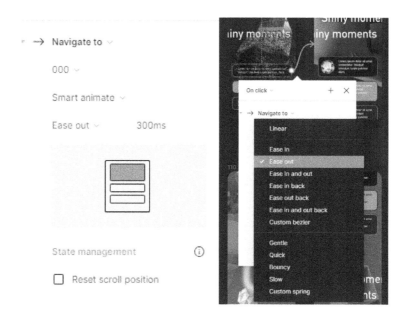

Easing refers to the way the computer interpolates or smoothly transitions between two keyframes. This is calculated using a mathematical function. Standardized Easing curves include Ease In, Ease Out, and Linear. More advanced easing options include Ease in Back, Ease Out Back, and Ease In and Out Back. You can also select custom to create custom Bezier easing curves. The duration controls the overall length of time for an animation in milliseconds. While over-flow behavior controls how users can interact with content that extends beyond the device's dimensions.

Easing and Curves

A well-tuned animation can bring your ideas and designs to life. Choose between Figma's easing presets or customize your own easing curve using the Bezier curve editor. Easing refers to the way the computer interpolates or smoothly transitions between two keyframes by using a mathematical function. This is represented by a curve and a graph, where time is applied to the X axis, and the animated attribute such as rotation, scale, or position is on the Y axis. A key frame is a point in time that indicates either the start or end of a change in an attribute, and is represented as points along the curve.

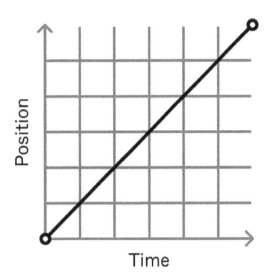

A Linear Ease is applied in a constant linear way, represented by a straight line. As objects in nature barely move at constant speed, linear curves can look unnatural or robotic.

When this is compared to the curved line of an Ease In transition, you get a much less robotic animation; an Ease In curve is when the interpolation starts slowly and accelerates as it reaches the end. It can feel sluggish but can work well for smoothly transitioning elements out of view.

Ease In

The opposite of an Ease In curve is an Ease Out curve, where the interpolation starts fast, and decelerates as it reaches the end. It can reinforce important visual information while still feeling responsive. It works well for transitioning elements into view.

Ease Out

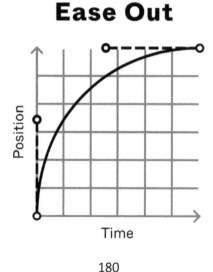

An Ease In and Out curve is when the interpolation starts slowly, accelerates in the middle, and decelerates at the end. For most motion, it feels smooth and responsive, but can feel unnatural and too perfect when applied to everything.

Ease In and Out

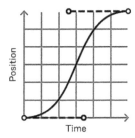

An Ease In Back curve is when the interpolation goes past the initial key frame value, and then accelerates as it reaches the end. This creates a bounce in the animation that serves as an anticipatory action, preparing the audience for, and reinforcing the main action. Much like Ease In. Ease In Back can work well for smoothly transitioning elements out of view.

Ease In Back

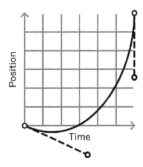

The Ease Out Back curve is the exact opposite of the Ease In Back curve; the interpolation starts fast, then decelerates and goes past the ending keyframe value before arriving at the ending keyframe. This creates a bounce in the animation that serves as a settlement, creating a smooth ending transition for the main action. Similar to Ease Out, Ease Out Back works for transitioning elements into view.

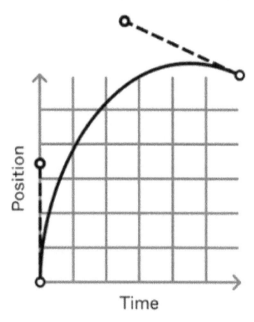

In an Ease In and Out Back curve, the interpolation starts slowly as it overshoots the initial key frame value, then accelerates quickly before decelerating and overshooting the ending key frame value, creating an anticipatory bounce at the start, a quick motion, and then a bounce settle at the end of the motion.

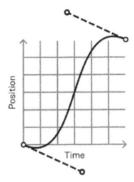

**Ease In And Out
Back Curve**

Position

Time

To apply an Ease and Curve to an animation, open the prototyping tab on the right side panel, then create or select any prototype in connection. You can apply Easing curves to any prototype animation except for Instant. In the animation section of the interaction details panel, you can find the Easing underneath the animation type.

→ Navigate to ⌄

000 ⌄

Smart animate ⌄

Ease out ⌄   300ms

State management   ⓘ

☐ Reset scroll position

To add more polish, you can create your own custom Easing curves by selecting the Custom option. This will open the Bezier curve editor. Create and edit custom Easing curves by clicking and dragging on each keyframe to create Bezier handles, or by adjusting the numerical values at the bottom of the panel. Copy and paste these numerical values to replicate an Ease.

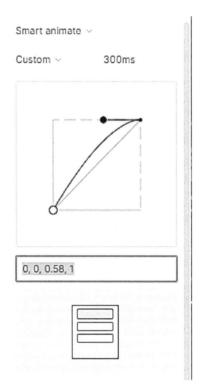

You can reset handles if they fall outside of the Bezier curve editor boundaries by clicking on the key frame or by entering 0,0 for the initial key frame and 1,1 for the ending key frame and the numerical values. Mousing over the preview window will display a preview of your animation.

Figma's Easing option adds polish to your prototype and brings your ideas and designs to life.

Smart Animate

Smart animate can map layers with matching names between two Figma frames and intelligently render animation frames between the two states. Smart animate is a surprisingly powerful animation tool that allows you to add motion and smooth transitions to your Figma prototype without having to add other tools like Adobe After Effects or Principle. It is typically used to transition between two screens in a proto-type.

Create a Loading Animation

Draw out an ellipse shape, and use the arc to have it cut in half. Use the ratio to turn it into a block arc.

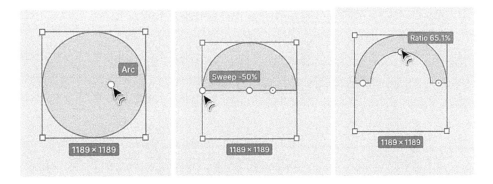

Next, use one of the arcs at the extreme to touch the other extreme to transform the shape into a donut. Then, reduce the thickness of the donut.

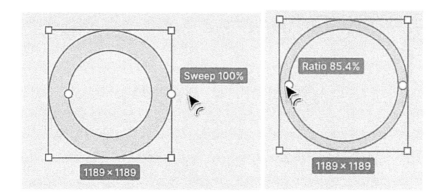

Duplicate (**Ctrl + D**) the donut, and reduce the duplicate to an arc size.

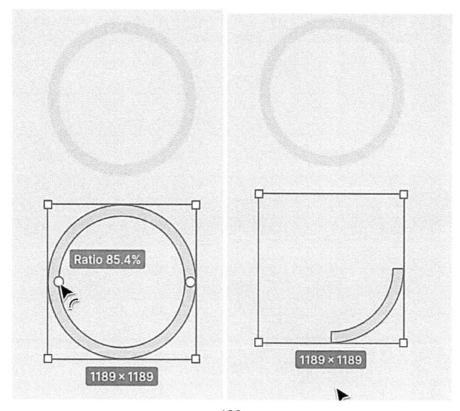

Next, select the arc duplicate, move over to the corner radius, and increase it until the arc has rounded end corners.

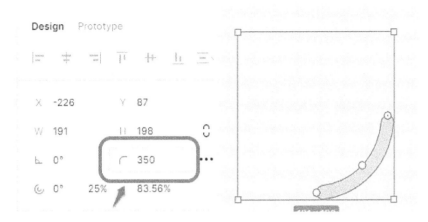

Now, change the color of the arc to blue. Next, turn the arc element into a frame, then select the frame, hold down your **Shift** key, and click on the original donut shape to bring it into the same frame as the arc.

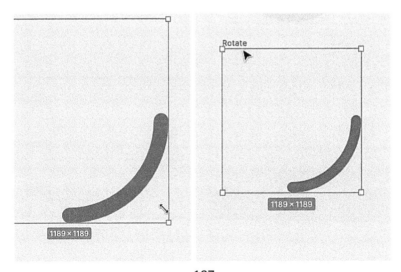

Now, with the frame still selected, go over to the Properties Design panel, and click on the Align Vertical Center option. This will cause the two elements to merge into one.

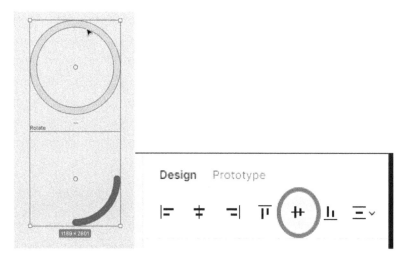

Next, click on the Create component option just above the canvas to turn the frame into a component.

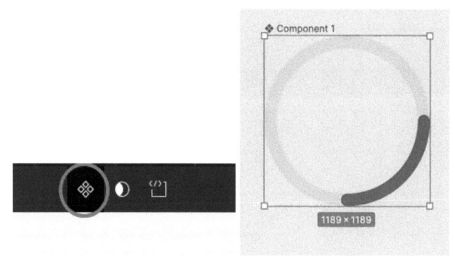

Now, click on the plus button below the dimension values to add a duplicate. Then make three more duplicates.

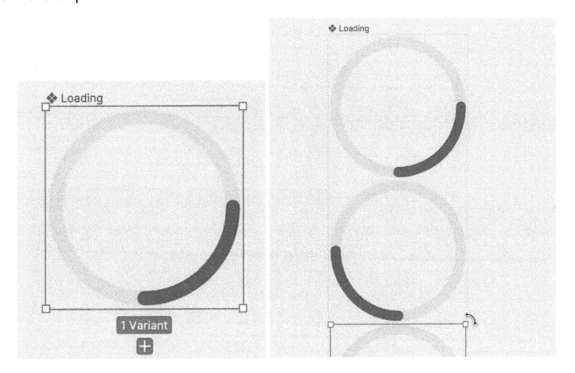

For each duplicate, change the position of the blue arc to the next 45-degree angle. Now, click on the prototype tab to start connecting them. Connect the first component to the one below it, and so on until the last one, then connect the last one back to the first one.

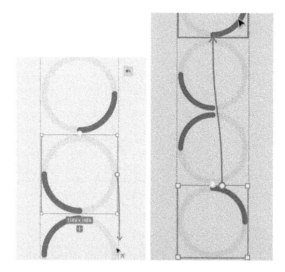

Now, click on all of the prototypes to select them, move over to the prototype interaction settings, and set them similar to the picture below.

Next, bring the frame of a mobile phone into your canvas. Then hold your Alt key and click and drag the first component into the phone's frame to create an instance of it inside.

Then, click on your presentation button to see your loading animation play out.

Importing and Exporting

Figma allows you to import files to the file browser or add assets to a design file.

Import to the File Browser

The file browser is where you view and manage your files.

From here, you can import Figma design files, sketch files, PNG images, JPEG images, mirror PDF etc. Anyone can use the file browser to import files into their drafts. If you have edit access to a team, you can also import files directly to projects within that team.

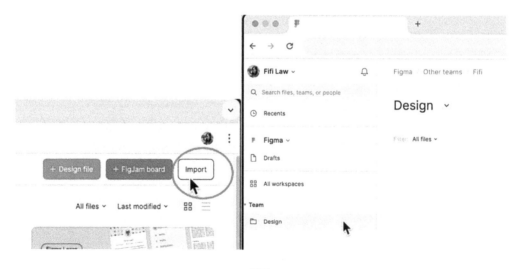

192

To import a file, click Import at the top right hand side of the file browser. Select *From your computer,* and then choose the files you want to import. You can select multiple files to import at the same time.

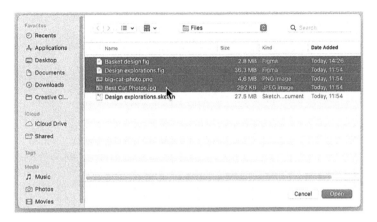

You can also drag and drop files from your computer into the file browser to import them.

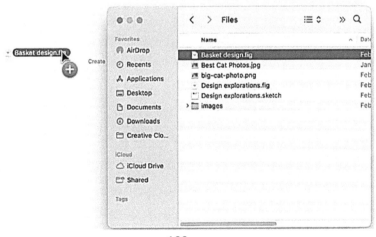

Once the import is complete, a new file is created that you can open and interact with, like other design files. If you are importing a very large Figma or sketch file, the import process may take up to several minutes. If you run into issues with import failing, consider breaking up the file pages into separate files and uploading them to Figma individually. When importing a Figma design or sketch file, keep in mind that the original file's version history and comments won't be included. Also, any further changes made to the original file will not be reflected in the imported file.

Import to the Design File

If you have edit access to a file, you can drag and drop images onto the canvas to import them. As long as a selected file is supported, Figma will add it to the canvas.

> **Supported file types:**
> - JPG
> - PNG
> - HEIC
> - WebP
> - GIF
> - SVG
> - TIFF (only on Safari)

When importing SVGs, keep in mind that they are no longer treated as images and are converted into Vector layers. If you are on a paid plan, you can also import MP4, MOB and WebM video files. You can also import assets using the Place image/video tool. To access this feature, open the shape tool dropdown in the toolbar and select *Place image/video*, or use the keyboard shortcut **Shift + Ctrl + K.**

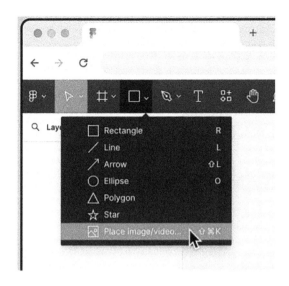

A window appears where you can select as many images or videos you want to add to the file. Once you are done selecting files, click *Open*.

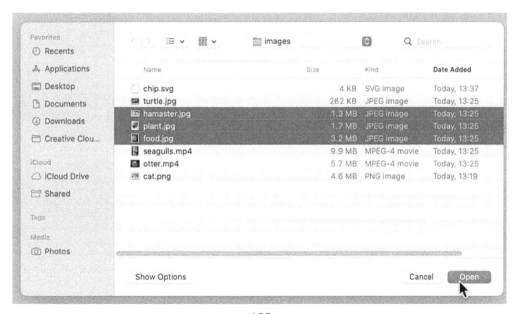

You will notice the cursor has changed to include a thumbnail that indicates how many files you selected and shows a preview of the first file that will be placed. To add assets to a specific area, navigate to their location and click on the canvas to place the file. Alternatively, you can click *Place All* in the toolbar to add all the files to a single location and reposition them afterwards.

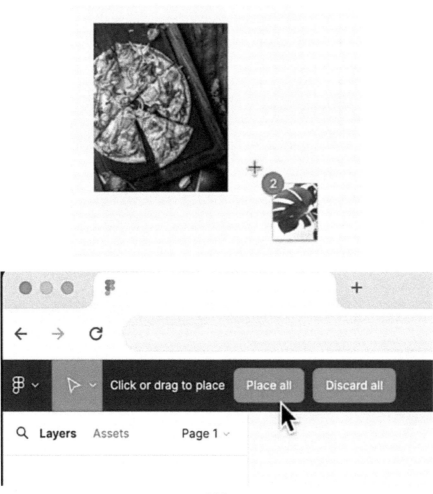

If you click the images on a shape or text layer, the asset will be applied as a fill. If you click inside a frame, the asset will be nested inside a frame layer.

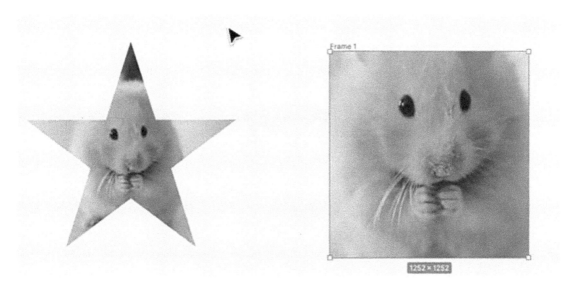

Exporting

Whether Figma is being used for work or for personal projects, it is important to know how to export content. You can export content to share with collaborators, facilitate the developer handoff, save copies of your work outside Figma, or for any other reason.

Export basics

You can export any layer type from Figma, like objects, groups, frames, and sections. To export a single object, select that object and use the export settings to apply an export configuration. Then, click the export button to export your object.

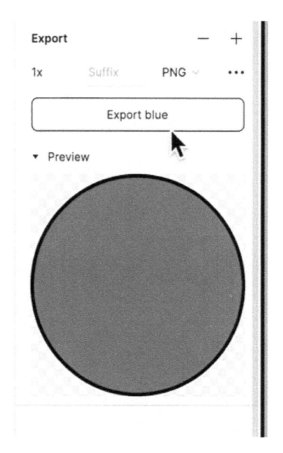

The location of the export section differs depending on the level of access to the file and the mode you are using. If you have edit access to the file and are in Design mode, the export section is located at the bottom of the design tab, as seen in the image above. If you have view access to a file and are in Design mode, you will find the export section on the Export tab in the right side bar. If you are using Dev mode, the Export section can be found on the Inspect tab in the right sidebar, but only if you have an object selected.

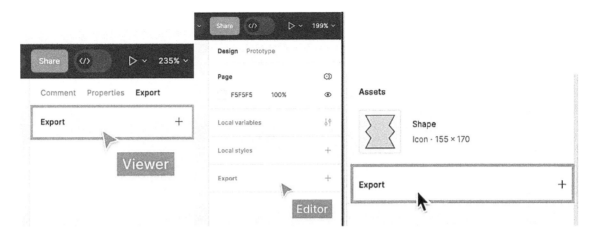

When the Export section cannot be found

If you are not seeing the Export section, the file owner has restricted you from being able to copy or export content. You will need to contact the file owner for assistance.

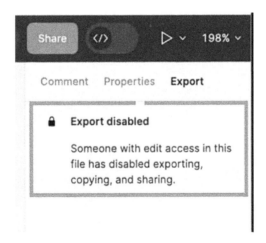

Exporting multiple objects

If you want to export multiple objects at the same time, simply select the objects by clicking and dragging your cursor over them, or by holding **Shift** and then clicking on each object. You can then use the export settings to add the same export configuration to each object simultaneously. When you export multiple objects like this, when you export multiple objects like this, they will each be exported to their own file. If you would rather export multiple objects to a single file, here are a few methods to use:

First up are groups and frames. To group objects, select the objects and use the keyboard shortcut (**Ctrl + G**) or right-click on one of the selected objects and choose *Group Selection*. Now, the object will be exported as a single file in the preview.

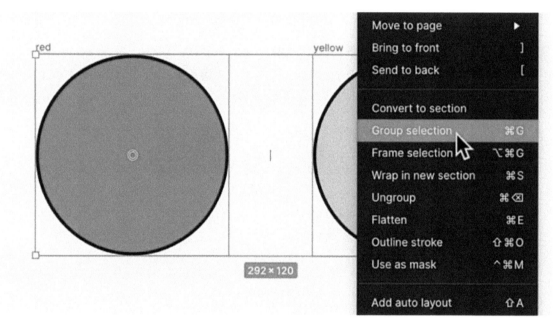

Like groups, frames also act as containers, allowing you to export all of the objects inside to a single file. To add objects to a frame, use the keyboard shortcuts (**Ctrl + alt + G**) or right click on a selected object and choose *Frame Selection*.

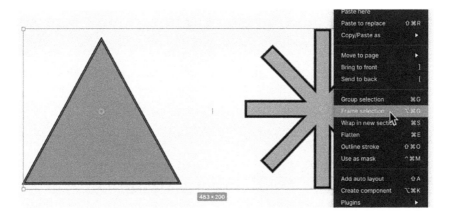

When exporting a frame with a fill, you can exclude the frame's fill from the exported file. To do this, select a frame with an export configuration and then deselect the Show in exports checkbox in the Fill section. Then, watch the preview change to a transparent background.

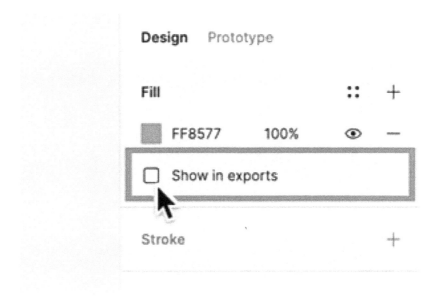

If you are an editor of the file, the export configuration you create will persist and be visible to others in the file. If you are just a viewer, your export configurations are not visible to others and do not persist after the file has been refreshed.

Why could frame content be excluded from the export?

When exporting a frame, keep in mind that only objects inside the frame will be exported. If you are running into issues with objects being left out of an export. Ensure that the layer is nested inside the frame in the layer's panel and not just visually on top of the frame on the canvas. Checking the export preview is also a great way to ensure that everything is where it needs to be.

Export with Section and Slice

Sections and slices can also be used to export objects to the same file in a way that won't impact your overall design. You can find both the Section and Slice tools under the Region tools drop down in the toolbar.

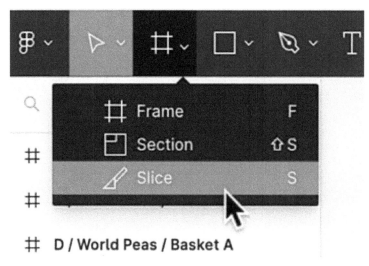

Sections are great for organizing objects on your canvas. With the Section tool selected, click and drag over existing objects to add them to a section. Looking at the left sidebar, you will see that the objects are nested within the section layer. Keep in mind that when you export a section, the section will include the section name and background fill.

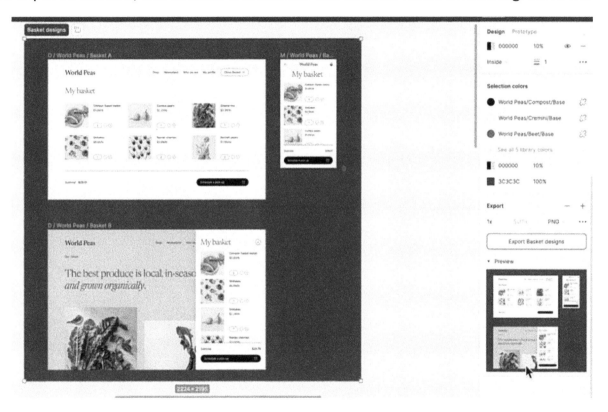

Slices are a bit different than sections. When you add a slice, you will notice a new object with a dashed border is added to your canvas.

You can move and resize the slice as needed, but only content inside the dashed borders will be included inside the export. Once you are done exporting, you can delete the slice layer.

Export an Entire Page

You can also export the entire canvas of the current page. To do this, deselect everything by clicking a blank spot on the canvas or by pressing the **Esc** key on your keyboard. Click the plus in the export section to add an export configuration. If you open the preview, you will see that the entire canvas will be included in the exported file.

Keep in mind that if your file has multiple pages, you will need to select and export content on each of those pages individually. If you no longer need an export configuration, simply click the minus sign next to it to have it removed.

When exporting an Entire File

You can always save your file as a local download of the file as a .Fig file, which is Figma's proprietary file format that can only be imported back into the Figma design. Keep in mind that the file's version history and any comments will not be included in the download file.

Customize your Export

Figma supports exporting content into PNG, JPG, SVG, and PDF files. The format will depend solely on your needs.

PNG (Portable Network Graphics) – PNG is a raster graphics format with color contrast, transparency, and lossless compression. When exporting, lossless compression preserves the original image quality and legibility of the text. Remember that exporting as a PNG will produce a file that is significantly larger than when exporting as a JPEG. PNGs are ideally suited for images with transparency and visuals that include both images and text, such as charts, logos, or illustrations.

Figma supports 32-bit PNGs with the RGBA color model. The A in RGBA stands for the alpha channel, which regulates a pixel's opacity. An alpha value is required in order to export PNG files.

JPG (Joint Photographic Group) - JPG, sometimes known as JPEG, is a lossy-compressed raster picture file format. Lossy compression shrinks file sizes by permanently eliminating data. This results in smaller files with lower image quality. In most circumstances, JPG quality is enough for web use and will minimize loading time due to its smaller size. JPG files can also be used for print design and photography. Keep in mind that JPGs do not support transparency, and compression can affect the reading of any text. If your image includes text or transparency, export it as a PNG or SVG instead.

SVG (Scalable Vector Graphics) – SVG is a vector graphics format based on XML. These are shapes based on numerical values and coordinates that can be displayed on any screen. SVGs are capable of scaling to any size without sacrificing image quality since they do not rely on pixels. They also value transparency. SVGs are commonly used in digital design because they may be represented in scripts or code. Use SVGs for logos, icons, and illustrations that you intend to include in responsive designs.

Things to keep in mind when exporting SVGs:

- Figma converts angular or diamond gradients into radial gradients.
- Background blur: You'll need to blur the layer directly.
- Text is automatically exported as glyphs. This implies you won't be able to alter the text layer after exporting. To maintain text editing, click and uncheck Outline Text.
- Figma exports strokes as fills.

PDF (portable Document Format) – PDFs enable you to share complex and interactive layouts. PDF files contain text, vector graphics, images, and typefaces in a fixed layout. PDFs allow you to render and alter individual design elements on any system. This makes it an adaptable format because it is unaffected by hardware, software, or operating systems.

Apple's mobile programming language, Xcode, supports PDF. This makes it an important tool for developing iOS applications. Use PDFs in Figma to export slide decks or share iOS development assets. They can also be used as print design mockups. Figma exports content as PDF 1.7 files.

Note that since Figma exports text as glyphs, there will be no text editing capability in the final PDF. You can still choose and copy text from the PDF when reading it in a browser or other suitable application.

In addition to the file type, there are some other options in the Export section. First, there is the scale option.

This determines the size of your export. With the scale set to 1x, the pixel value of the export will be the same as the one listed on the sidebar. If the scale is changed to 3x, those pixel values would triple. Keep in mind that if you are exporting content to a PDF or SVG, the scale can only be set to 1x.

In addition to the default scale options in the dropdown, you can also manually enter a custom scale. To export at a custom multiplier, enter a number in the scale field. To export at a fixed width or height, enter a number followed by **W** or **H,** respectively.

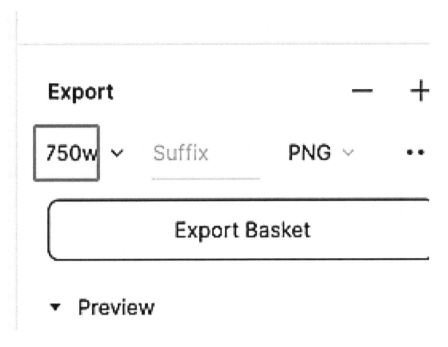

By default, content exported from Figma has a Dots Per Inch (DPI) of 72. And images DPI increases as the scale increases. To calculate the DPI of an image exported at scale, multiply 72 by the chosen scale (i.e 72 x 2 = 144). If you are exporting content for high-density screens like retina displays, it is a good practice to export your design at 2x your intended asset resolution.

Next to the scale option is the Suffix field. By default, exported files have the same name as the layer you are exporting. The export button gives you a preview of what the exported file name will be. You can use a Suffix field to add labels to the end of the file name. This can help you organize your export without having to change the layers names in the file. For instance, if you enter '—active' in the Suffix field, the exported file will be named button-active.png

When you are happy with your export configuration, click Export. The exported file will be sent to the download location in your browser preferences.

Exporting in Variant

When exporting in variant, the variant properties are often used for the file name. To help you stay more organized when exporting in variant, the exported file name will use more variant properties and their values than the layer name. For instance, if you export a variant with a Type = Primary, and State = Default.

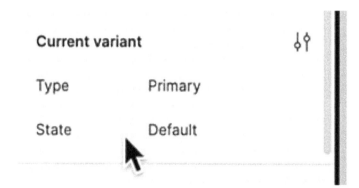

Your exported file will be named Type = Primary, State = Default. To avoid this, consider exporting an instance of the variant instead.

Multiple Export Configurations

In some cases, you may want to export an object at multiple scales or in different file formats. You can apply as many export configurations to an export as needed. Simply click the plus in the Export section to add another export configuration. Notice that

Figma automatically sets the New export configuration scale to 2x and adds @2x to the Suffix field, but you can modify the value to fit your needs.

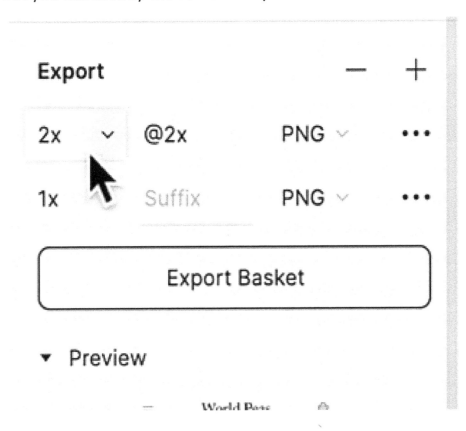

Bulk Export

If you want to export multiple objects that already have an export configuration set, consider using the bulk export list instead. To access the bulk export list, go to the *Main Menu*, then *File*, and click *Export*. Otherwise, you can use the Keyboard shortcut **Shift + Ctrl + E**.

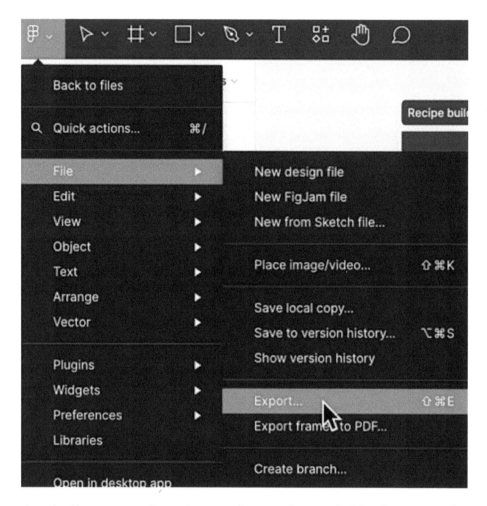

By default, the bulk export list shows the scale and file format of every export configuration set on your current page. To narrow down this option ahead of time, select the object you want to export before opening the bulk export list. Clicking on the configuration thumbnail brings you to that object on your canvas. Deselect the box for any selections you don't want to export, and then click Export.

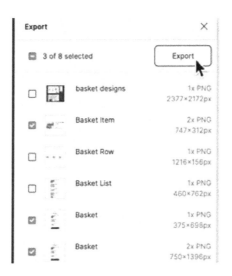

Plugins in Figma

Plugins enhance your Figma experience; they are like peanut butter to your jelly. The programs built by the community extend the functionality of Figma and FigJam. Plugins are valuable pieces of software that let anyone contribute and customize Figma to fit every workflow. Figma's community has hundreds of plugins that you can install with a single click. You can run installed plugins within a file without interrupting your flow. Want to animate repetitive tasks like designing responsive breakpoints? *Responsify* (by Brian Lovin) and *Breakpoints* (by Floweare) are examples of plugins that are sure to help you get around that. If you need a quick way to replace placeholder content with real data, Plugins like *Content Reel* by the team at Microsoft can help you get this done in no time. Plugins like *Mapsicle* let you access a third party API, so you can insert realistic maps into your file.

Some plugins also have a relaunch button, so teammates can relaunch the plugin later and make adjustments as we all collaborate together. Plugins even let you play games in Figma, like Kevin Kwok's *Multiplayer Pong Game*. If you cannot find the plugin you desire, you can as well work towards building one for yourself, your team, and the Figma community in order to help others get ahead too.

CHAPTER EIGHT
FIGMA TIPS AND TRICKS

Efficiency is essential for a product designer who wants to meet deadlines and deliver high-quality work. Figma, a well-known design program, provides a number of effective features to improve workflow efficiency. Mastering keyboard shortcuts is one of the most efficient strategies to increase your productivity in Figma.

Keyboard Shortcut

Selection Shortcuts

- o **V**: Select the "Move" tool.
- o **K**: Select 'Scale' tool.
- o **Ctrl/Cmd + A**: Select all elements on the canvas.
- o **Shift + Click**: Add or remove an element from the current selection.
- o **Ctrl/Cmd + G**: Group selected objects.
- o **Ctrl/Cmd + Shift + G**: Ungroup selected objects.
- o **Shift + A**: Apply Auto Layout to selected objects.

Zooming/Navigation Shortcut

- o **Spacebar**: Temporarily select the "Hand" tool for panning around the canvas.

- Ctrl/Cmd + Plus (+): To Zoom in.
- Ctrl/Cmd + Minus (-): To Zoom out.

Layer Organization Shortcuts

- **Ctrl/Cmd + G**: To Group selected layers.
- **Ctrl/Cmd + Shift + G**: To Ungroup selected layers.
- **Ctrl/Cmd + D**: To Duplicate selected layer(s).
- **Ctrl/Cmd + Shift + L**: To Lock selected layer(s).
- **Ctrl/Cmd + Shift + L**: To Unlock selected layer(s).
- **Ctrl/Cmd + Alt + T**: Tidy Up – Align and distribute elements in your design with one click.

Editing Shortcuts

- **Ctrl/Cmd + C**: Copy selected layer(s).
- **Ctrl/Cmd + V**: Paste copied layer(s).
- **Ctrl/Cmd + X**: Cut selected layer(s).
- **Ctrl/Cmd + Z**: Undo the last action.
- **Ctrl/Cmd + Shift + Z**: Redo the last action.
- **Ctrl/Cmd + Shift + R**: Paste to replace (maintains the original position of the copied layer).

Prototyping Shortcuts

- **Tab**: Navigate between interactive elements in prototype mode.
- **Shift + Tab**: Navigate backward between interactive elements.
- **Ctrl/Cmd + Option + Enter**: Preview prototype.

- o **Shift + D**: Toggle ON Dev mode.
- o **Ctrl + X**: Quickly toggle between Fixed and Auto Spacing
- o **Ctrl + B**: Toggle align text space line

Keyboard shortcuts are quite useful for speeding up your design process in Figma. By learning these useful shortcuts, you may dramatically increase your productivity and save time. These shortcuts help you complete a wide range of tasks faster, from selection and navigation to editing and prototyping.

Tips and Tricks

Crop Images: Although a mask is good for advance cropping, here is something you can do to quickly crop an image. Click on the image, hold down **Ctrl/Cmd**, and drag the edges of the image to crop them out. To make such cropping even on both sides, hold down the **Alt** button as well (**Ctrl + Alt**).

Math Operation: You can perform math operations directly on your design panel right there. If, for instance, you have a rectangle in a frame that is 750 in width and you want to make the rectangle half of that frame, simply go over to the Width (W) in the design panel and type 750/2, then hit enter. You can also do this with multiplication, addition, and subtraction. These math operations will help you simplify your task of moving things and adjusting positions.

Nudge Value: When you select a frame or an element and use the arrow keys, it moves it by one pixel. For instance, if you are using a grid system, the default nudge value is always 10 on Figma. For that, you just hold Shift and use the arrow keys to move. However, how the element moves on the canvas using the arrow keys can be increased. Simply go to Figma *Main Menu > Preferences > Nudge* amount. In the dialog box that will pop up, you can change it to whatever value you want.

Nudge amount		✕
Small nudge	Big nudge	
1	10	

Distance between Elements: If you want to find the distance between elements, select the first element, hold down Alt on your keyboard, and hover over the different elements, and the distance with respect to each element will appear.

Duplicate Last Action: This is very useful when repeating a particular pattern. For instance, if you duplicate an element and position it just below the original,. Now, when you hit **Ctrl + D**, it duplicates it in the manner of action that you performed previously. This way, you can easily create the grid or pattern you wish to create.

Copy and Paste Properties: Quickly copy and paste styles and properties from one element to another in your design. This can be helpful when creating a lot of screens. When you have an element with several styling properties in it, simply select and hit **Alt + Ctrl + C/V (C = Copy**, **V = Paste**). You can also right click *Copy/Paste as > Copy* *properties*. Then select the next element, and then use the shortcut or follow the same right click to paste the properties.

Ignore Constraints While Resizing: There will be different scenarios where you want to resize a particular frame, but there are different elements inside it that have constraints that lead to different breaks within the elements. To ignore this constraint, simply hold **Ctrl/Cmd** while resizing the frame.

Set File Thumbnails: This helps in organizing things on your dashboard. For example, there are different files that just show the frames or a quick overview of your files. And this isn't helpful to quickly navigate to different files, the best thing to do is to set an image as the thumbnail of the file, in order to enable you to easily identify it amongst the many files you have. To do this, simply open that particular file, then on the canvas, select the frame that you want to use as a thumbnail, right-click on it, and then you have the option to *Set as thumbnail.*

Copy as PNG: This comes in handy when you want to copy a particular frame or a screen and send it to someone on Slack, Microsoft Teams, Email or WhatsApp. All you need to do is select a frame, then use the shortcut **Shift + Ctrl + C,** and it gets copied to your clipboard. Otherwise, you can right-click on the frame and select *Copy/Paste as > Copy as PNG*. Now that it is on your keyboard, you can place it anywhere on your system.

Change Text Resizing: In a situation where you have your text wrapping into another line and you would like to have it resized, rather than stretching the text frame or moving over to the Text section in the Design panel, simply move your cursor to the edge of the frame and do a double-click to change the text resizing to auto width.

Hide Controls: This is helpful when presenting something and screen sharing with colleagues or clients. Use the shortcut **Ctrl + Dot** (.) to change it into a full view and allow you to share screen for a presentation. Repeat the shortcut to bring back the controls.

Collapse Layers: A useful tip to quickly collapse all layers to find parent frames. Simply use the keyboard shortcut **Alt + L** to collapse every layer and help you find a particular frame.

Add Links: This can come in handy when you want to jump to a particular resource or externally. So if you have a website link that you want to link to, simply go to the page you created and want to link to, then right-click and *Copy/Paste as > Copy link* to generate a link for that page and have it copied to the click board. Then move over to the other page where you have a particular text you wish to be converted to a link. Select the text, and just above the canvas is a link icon that reads Create link. Click on it to add a link, and you can also use the shortcut **Ctrl + K**. This will give you a small input field, then paste the link you just copied from the other page. Now you have just added a link to the text that will take the user to a different page.

Multi Paste: This comes in very handy if you want to paste a particular element onto multiple frames at once. Simply select all the frames and use the **Ctrl + V** shortcut to paste them to the various frames selected. And with the selection in place, you can move it to a different location, but by default, the element gets pasted onto the center of a particular frame.

'Magician' Plugin: This plugin works around the text edit feature. It allows you to type in a piece of text and convert the text into better text. If you are one who writes headings or any form of UX copy, this will help out a lot.

Name Multiple Layers: If you want to rename multiple layers or multiple frames at the same time, select all the layers you want to rename, hit **Ctrl + R**, and this will pop up a rename dialog box.

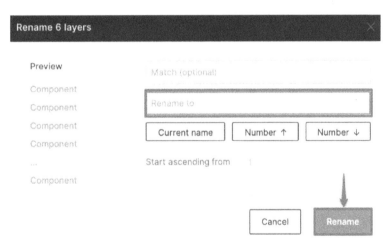

You can select what names it should match with; otherwise, you can just give it a general name. Also, the number descending or number ascending option will determine what the number sequence will be, if there are any. Then click Rename when you are done.

Quick Color Names: When dealing with colors, you don't need to remember the hex values for all the colors. You can actually put color names in the Fill section of the Design tab, and whatever element is selected will change to that color. Anytime it fails to give the typed in color due to a typo error, an invalid name, or whatever else might be the case, it will resort back to the default gray.

Emoji File Hack: Emojis can be used in so many ways, and Figma now allows us to use them when renaming files, layers, and elements. The good thing about this, is that the emoji also shows up wherever the names are stored.

Auto Layout Hack: When you have a component or element inside an auto layout frame, you can change between *Fill* or *Hug* real quick. All you need to do is hold down **Alt** or **Option** on your keyboard and double click on one of the edges of the element. These work vice versa, too. For the parent frame, hold down **Ctrl** or **Cmd** on your keyboard and double clicking on one of the edges.

Help and Resource button: This button is one of the most underrated in Figma. It is located at the bottom right corner of your screen. It consists of very useful options, one of which is the complete keyboard shortcut view that reveals every keyboard shortcut you need, and every one of them has been arranged into different categories.

You can as well change your keyboard layout if you wish to, right from there.

Drag to Change: We often change the size of elements from the properties panel. However, you can drag to increase or decrease any property size if it is in a number format. All you need to do is select your element and hover your cursor over the edge of the size option in the properties panel (W, H, Y, X, etc.) This will cause your cursor to switch to a double headed arrow facing apart. Now, click and drag that arrow left or right to modify the value of the size aspect that you clicked.

Special GIF Support: With Figma GIF support, you can drag in a GIF into your canvas, and click on the Play Presentation button to have your GIF play out. This is brilliant because it can be used with any Lottie based animation as well, as long as it ends with.GIF, which is the GIF format.

CHAPTER NINE
FIGJAM IN FIGMA

FigJam is an online collaboration tool that allows you and your team to explore, create, and organize ideas. You don't need any prior experience of design tools to begin jamming. FigJam files are lightweight, inclusive ecosystems in which everyone may participate. Consider them digital whiteboards where you and your team may:

- Brainstorm and explore ideas
- Create decision trees, diagrams, and mind maps
- Conduct design critiques and feedback
- Collect ideas, note feedback, and organize research
- Plan and run meetings, tutorials, and interactive sessions
- Collaborate and align with project stakeholders in one place.

FigJam is designed for remote teams to work together in real time, and it includes features such as sticky notes, shapes, and connectors. FigJam is not intended for creating high-fidelity designs/wireframes but rather for facilitating collaboration and communication among team members.

Figma vs FigJam

Figma and FigJam are both products developed by Figma, but they serve different purposes. FigJam has been specially built to help you ideate and brainstorm rather than design UI or other digital products (i.e., websites), which is what Figma is for. Also, FigJam has a limited tool set that helps you focus and get into those tasks.

Figma is a vector drawing tool where you can use the pen tool to create your own custom vector shape. And because everything in Figma is vector and you are drawing on a pixel scale, you can increase and decrease the size of your design, which will maintain scale and quality. FigJam, on the other hand, is more of a whiteboarding tool, similar to tools like Miro. FigJam does not support vectors, so you can't draw your own custom shapes or use the pen tool. Also, there are a limited number of shapes that you can create in FigJam. While you are limited to a set of shapes and text functionality in FigJam. They also support things like stickers, emojis, and reactions. There are also a few plugins and widgets that can be helpful. FigJam has a range of templates to help you get started, but you can also copy and paste your cover from Figma into FigJam, but they will be pasted as a flattened image, so you wouldn't be able to see individual layers or vectors that make up that design.

Both of these tools have commenting and collaboration features because they all kind of build up in the browser.

When should I use which tool?

Although both tools are similar in some way, their key differences make them have different purposes, and each can shine at different parts of the design process. FigJam being more of a low-fidelity whiteboarding tool is most valuable in discovery work and exploration, where one will intentionally want to keep things low-fidelity. In this way, it can be used to kick off a project, do workshops, and run sprints, where the focus is more on the ideation than the execution. It is also a great way to gather and vote on ideas.

Also, it is mostly common knowledge that running workshops and exercises involve timelines, so there are often different timers for different exercises during workshops. And FigJam has a built in timer at the top left corner, where you can start the timer for as long as you want, and everybody who is in that FigJam file can see the timer and know how much time is left.

Another important thing that can be done at the FigJam stage is research – synthesizing research and bringing in quotes or insight during user testing, of which the post-it notes get really useful, all of which will aid in organizing information. Also, functions can easily be created with FigJam because it has all the built-in shapes, flows, and arrows needed to create your final flow.

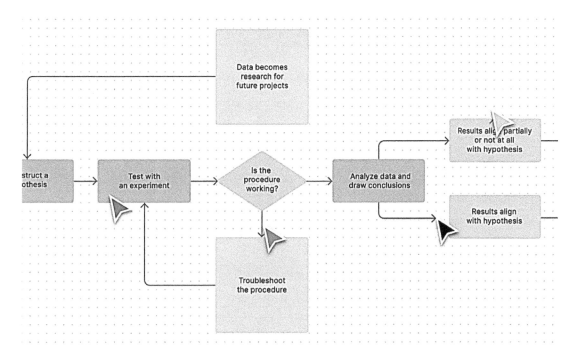

Doing it in FigJam with this level of fidelity also helps you be more focused on the functional part of your flow rather than getting caught up in the wireframes and visuals that are contained in Figma.

The second phase of refinement, polish, and handoff is where Figma really starts to excel. Often, during this part of the work, you are getting more into that high-fidelity stage of the work by starting to refine the designs and maybe even create a few prototypes at this stage. As you are designing screens, you would want to have access to those robust drawing and vector drawing capabilities so you can create your own custom shapes and really manipulate the design to look exactly how you want it.

Figma also supports design libraries, so you can turn on a design library for your team or company, and easily pull in assets, components, and variants that you need to put in your designs to fit within the design system. If you have a few designs that you want to bring to a user testing session and get some feedback from potential customers or users, this is where Figma is really great, because you can actually turn those designs into interactive prototypes.

Figma has a lot of robust built-in prototyping features and capabilities, like setting your interactions, transitions, and scrollable views on your page, as well as fixing content to the page as it scrolls. Figma lets you create multiple prototypes on one page or in one file, so that way you could have a few different flows that you may want to test in a user testing session, and it's all there in one place. Figma lets you quickly create a share link that you can then share with potential users that you are going to be wanting to do the user testing with, so they can open it up in their browser and actually click through and interact with your prototype. This stage of the work is often where you create presentations to give feedback and updates on how the project is going.

One common exercise that teams should do at this stage is a retro. Which is basically a retrospective, looking back at how the project went. This retro is best run in FigJam, and this is not only because FigJam is a better tool, but it is also a little bit more inclusive of all of the people participating in the retrospective. So, usually, it is not just the designers engaging in this exercise; everyone else is also working on this project and the team. That will see non-designers coming in to participate in the retro, and FigJam is just a little easier to use for people who don't necessarily have robust drawing design tool experience.

So in FigJam, you find a built-in retrospective template which you can use to reflect on what went well and what didn't go well, and to generate new ideas on what to do right and do things differently.

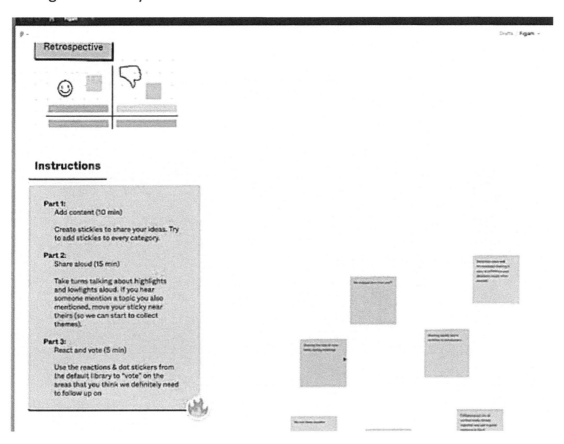

With all that has been said, it can be seen that both tools have unique functionality and capabilities that can be used at different moments in the design process.

Creating a FigJam File

FigJam is accessed through Figma. You may find them along-side your standard design files in your teams, projects, and drafts. Using the file browser, create a new FigJam file from any file creation point. Launch Figma from the file browser.

Go to the sidebar and select Recents or Drafts. Select + on the FigJam board at the upper right of the screen. Alternatively, open the file browser and navigate to a project. To add a new board to the project, click the FigJam board.

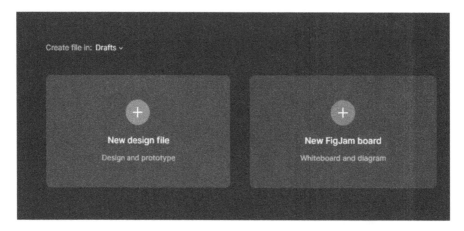

There are three separate sections in FigJam files: the board, the file toolbar, and the objects bar and main tools.

The Canvas/Board

When you open a new FigJam file, you get presented with a giant, unlimited, infinite blank canvas.

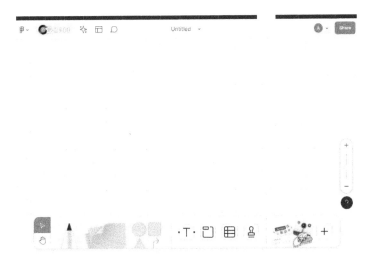

Sections help you contain, cluster, and move things on your board. There are two methods for creating a segment ⬜ on your board:

Toolbar – Click on the Section icon ⬜ on the toolbar or use the shortcut **Shift + S**.

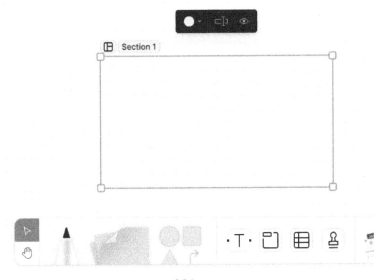

To make a square section, click where you want the section to be placed on the board, or click-and-drag to create a custom size section. Additionally, you can drag and drop a section over the elements you wish to include in it.

Selection - Click and drag things on the board to add them to a section. Right-click the selection. Select Create Section from the menu.

Stickies

Stickies are a virtual version of the popular sticky notes. They are the foundation of any FigJam board, together with shapes and connectors. Click the sticky notes in the toolbar, then select the color you want, drag it into the section, and start typing.

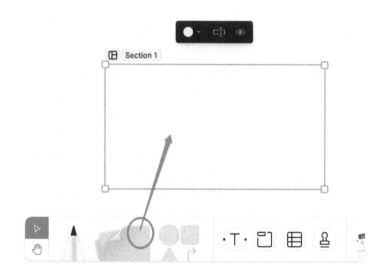

Stickies that you add to the board will by default have your name on them, but you can choose to remove this by clicking on the feather icon from the properties option when the sticky is selected.

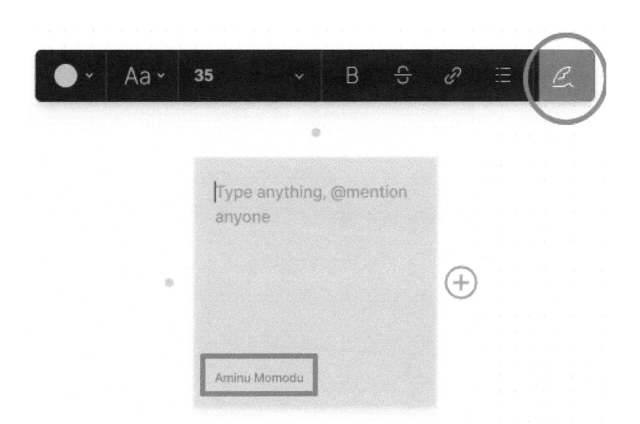

Shapes, Connectors and Lines

Shapes in FigJam are an essential tool for any project. Shapes can be scaled, rotated, and given solid or dashed outlines. Shapes are ideal for diagrams, user journeys and flows, flow charts, and a variety of other uses. There are several ways to build a shape, including using the toolbar or an existing shape on the board.

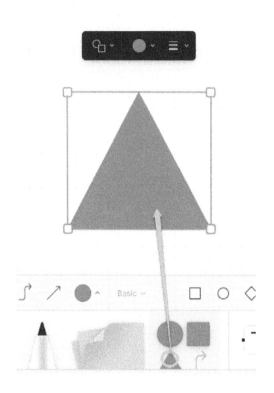

To bring in a shape, you can click on the shape tool to select a shape, then go over a spot on the canvas to draw the shape. You can also drag and drop a shape from the toolbar to the canvas.

Connect stickies to construct flow diagrams or trails for others to follow. Click on the ✐ toolbar. Choose between an elbow or a straight connector. To construct an elbow connection, click **X** or **Shift + L**, and just **L** creates a straight connection. To link two objects, move your mouse between them by clicking and dragging.

After you've constructed a connector, you may click and drag its start or end point to another item or another side of the same one.

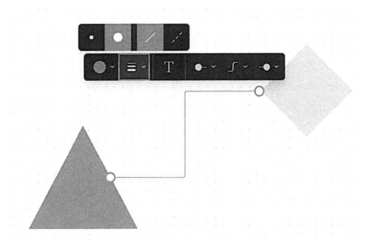

The connector or straight line can also be modified by color, start/end point, and thickness.

Draw and Highlight

Use the FigJam highlighter, marker, and washi tape tools to draw on the board and other items. It's a wonderful way to express your personality, draw attention to anything on the canvas, or doodle something creative.

Doodle – To create your next masterpiece with the marker tool:

- o Select the marker tool from the toolbar by clicking or pressing the **M** key.
- o Choose a hue and thin or thick stroke weight. You can always modify this after you've completed your doodle.
- o Doodle by clicking and dragging on the board.
- o To add structure to your doodles, hold **Shift** and draw a straight line.

The marker tool will remain active until you select another tool or click **Esc**. By default, the marker creates a narrow, gray stroke.

Highlighter – To highlight your board, follow these steps:

- o Click the drawing tool in the toolbar and select the highlighter, or press **Shift + M**.
- o Choose a color and stroke weight, which can be changed later.
- o Click and drag on the board to draw a highlight.
- o Hold **Shift** to highlight in a straight line.

Washi Tape - To apply washi tape:

- o Click the sketching tools menu and choose washi tape, or press **W**.
- o Choose a washi tape design or click ⊕ to upload an image.
- o Click and drag the tape to a desired location on the board.

Add Text

Text is an essential tool for scribbling down ideas while brainstorming and conveying information with others. Text can be added to the board by clicking in the toolbar or pressing the **T** ·T· key. Text objects are used to place text on top of other objects or straight onto the board.

Single click

A single click generates a text box that resizes horizontally as you input it, often known as point text. A text box's width can be adjusted by dragging the sides. Choose the text tool or hit the **T** key. Create a text box by ·T· clicking anywhere on the board.

Click and drag

Create a text box by clicking and dragging it to the next line, wrapping any horizontal overflow content. This is also referred to as area text. The item has a set width and expands vertically as you add text. Click and hold anywhere on the board. Drag your pointer to add a text layer with precise dimensions.

Use Templates

With templates, your team may start working on new or current files with pre-made material that provides direction and building blocks. To help your team add tasks and goals as stickies, the Daily Standup template, for instance, adds premade columns to your board. A matrix for evaluating the viability and importance of ideas for a project is included in the Prioritization Matrix Template, along with sections set out for brainstorming.

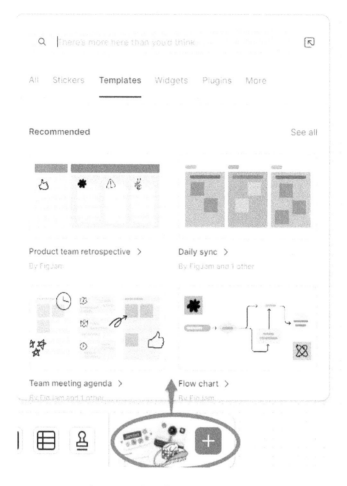

- Move your cursor over the stack of recently used toolbar icons.
- To bring up the modal, click the More button.
- Select the Templates tab.
- Scroll and browse the various templates, or use the search bar at the top of the modal to find a specific keyword.
- Hover over a template and select Add Template to add it to your board.

Import Objects

Add images – You can import static photos in PNG, JPEG, GIF, TIFF, HEIC, and WEBP formats, as well as animated images in GIF format. Static images do not animate. The following static image formats are supported: PNG, JPEG, GIF, TIFF, HEIC, and WEBP.

To include an image:

- Hover over the list of recently used icons in your toolbar and select More. Choose the More option.
- Choose images.
- Select a picture from your PC.

Figma paste design – Copy and paste layers from Figma into FigJam. This includes frames, photos, components, text layers, links, and more. Because FigJam files lack a layer's panel, you will have fewer options when selecting frames, components, or other layers transferred from Figma design files.

Link text – Add clickable links to text that references Figma files, FigJam files, documentation, or external websites. Choose an object or a particular string of text. Click or use this keyboard shortcut: **Ctrl/Cmd + K**. Enter or paste the URL from the clipboard.

If you already have the URL copied to your clipboard, select the text and press **Ctrl/Cmd + V** to insert your link.

Import spreadsheet data - Drag and drop the CSV file into your board to import it, or:

- o Click on the toolbar at the top.
- o Select Import from CSV under File.
- o Click Open after selecting a CSV file.

Additionally, you can directly copy and paste spreadsheet cells onto your board. The information in the CSV cells is transformed into a FigJam table once the import is finished.

Note - Tables can only contain 500 cells. Only the first 500 cells of data will be imported if the amount in your CSV files exceeds the restriction. Think about creating additional tables if you want to contribute more than 500 cells of data to FigJam.

<u>Convert table to stickies</u> – Convert cells in a table into stickies by first selecting the table, then opening the Quick Actions with the shortcut **Ctrl + P**. Type 'convert to stickies' and hit **Enter**.

Collaborate During Meetings

Comments, chat, and mentions – To write 🗩 a comment on the board, click or hit **C**. When modifying a text field, use **@** to tag someone in your file. To show a temporary message in a file using your multiplayer cursor, press **/** and begin typing.

Stamps and emotes - Stamps are curated stickers that you can apply on a board or other item to convey comments. How to apply stamps:

- Either click 🔖 on the toolbar or use the shortcut key **E** on the keyboard.
- Select the desired stamp by clicking on it on the stamp wheel.
- To insert the stamp, click on the board or an object.

Emotes are brief bursts of emoji reactions. To employ emotes, click on the emote tool. There are several approaches to this:

- Using a right-click, choose emote on the board.
- Click ✦ then choose "Emote."
- Click 🔖 to switch to the emote wheel while the stamp wheel is open.

Select the desired emote by clicking on it on the emote wheel. A blast of emotes can be released by clicking anywhere on the board. To emit a continuous stream of emotes, click and hold.

If you haven't emoted in a long time, FigJam slowly fades into emote mode and returns you to the select tool. To close the emote tool, you can alternatively hit **Esc**.

Use stickers and Figma libraries - You can add stickers and components made by your team and other Figma Community members to your board using the libraries available in FigJam.

To look through your library collections:

o Hover over the list of recently used icons in your toolbar and select the More button to launch the modal.
o Click the **Stickers** tab.
o Search for decals and parts, or go through your library.
o Drag and drop an object from the library onto your board.

You could as well use the shortcut **Alt + 2** to open the modal.

Audio call – Click 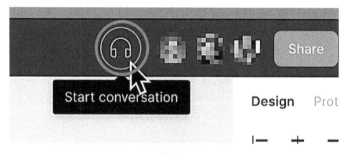 in the toolbar to initiate or participate in a conversation. When there is a green outline surrounding the avatars, a conversation is in progress.

Click Join to become a part of an ongoing discussion.

Spotlight yourself – When you spotlight yourself, all contributors viewing a work are told that you have asked them to follow you. This is useful for doing workshops and meetings in FigJam and Figma design over audio discussions.

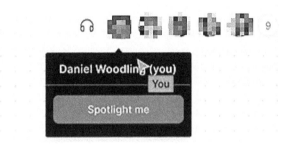

To do a spotlight, hover over your avatar in the top toolbar of a Figma or FigJam design file. Select "Spotlight me."

Everyone who is presently reading the file will now be informed that you would like them to follow you. They have a few seconds to ignore your request before seeing your view of the file.

Create and Publish Template

Custom templates allow you to quickly add content to FigJam files without having to create the file from scratch. Whether you want to express your team's style or document its special procedures and traditions, you may make templates that do just that.

A custom template for a FigJam file can be created and published by any member of your organization with edit access. For a FigJam file to be published as a template:

- Click the Share icon in the top toolbar.
- Click Publish as a template after selecting the Publish tab. FigJam will ask you to move the file to a project if it is currently in your drafts.
- Provide the template with a name, description, and thumbnail image.
- Choose if you wish to publish to your present team or to your organization.
- Anyone in your organization can use it if it is set up in your organization.
- The template can only be used by members of the team that the file is on if it is set to the current team.
- Click Publish.

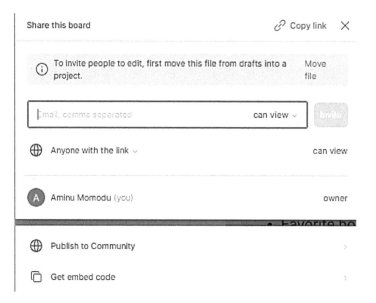

About the Author

Anthony Sanchez is a seasoned UX/UI designer with a passion for crafting seamless digital experiences. With a background in both design and writing, he brings a unique perspective to his work, ensuring that every interaction feels intuitive and engaging. His expertise lies in leveraging Figma to translate complex design concepts into clear, concise copy that guides users through interfaces with ease.

Having worked on numerous projects across various industries, Sanchez understands the importance of clear communication in enhancing user interactions. His expertise in Figma allows him to seamlessly integrate content into the design process, ensuring cohesive and user-friendly digital experiences.

As an advocate for user-centered design principles, Sanchez is passionate about empowering designers and writers alike to collaborate effectively and create impactful solutions. Through his writing, workshops, and online resources, he aims to share practical insights and best practices for leveraging Figma as a powerful tool for UX/UI design.

Anthony Sanchez is excited to share his knowledge and expertise with readers, offering actionable advice and strategies for elevating their design workflows and delivering exceptional user experiences.

www.ingramcontent.com/pod-product-compliance
Lightning Source LLC
Chambersburg PA
CBHW041007050326
40690CB00031B/5292